Matthew Thomp

GW00792191

THE
BLOOD
TIPPED
BLADE

How To Fight **Porn** Addictions In
Generation XXX

I was 11 years old.

My name is Matthew Thompson. I'm a 23-year-old from Belfast, Northern Ireland, and I was addicted to pornography from 11 to 16 years old.

I say *I was* because as you'll read in the following pages I was able to overcome this addiction (as can you).

The road to freedom was the hardest journey of my life, but it was also the most worthy.

At the time of publishing, my beautiful wife Jaci and I will be married for two years, and I will have been 'sober' for seven.

Growing up I never believed either of those two things would ever be possible. I thought I was destined to be stuck in a cycle forever and be 'forever alone' because of it.

But this secret was destroying my world and taboos will always remain taboos unless people stand up and speak out.

This book is unlike anything else you have ever read, and I can't promise you will like it.

It may shock you, it may make you angry, and you definitely won't agree with everything it has to say.

But I can promise that in it you'll find radical vulnerability and the truth about what many young men and women face today.

It's my prayer that this little book changes your life, but if it doesn't at least you'll know that **you are not alone.**

What is pornography?

Everyone has a different experience with porn.

No 2 stories are the same, therefore, for the purposes of this book the term 'porn' will be used quite broadly.

It'll be interchangeable with lust, masturbation, hooking up, fantasizing etc.

This has a two-fold purpose:
1. It saves me having to write out every single variation of lust every time.
2. It can become an umbrella term for you to inject your own story into.

I admit this may seem like an odd approach, so here are some examples of what I mean:

Reading erotic fiction could be just as much 'pornography' to one person as watching an XXX hardcore video is to another.

Having a sexual daydream can be 'porn' in the same way obsessing over a pornographic magazine can be.

For some, allowing our eyes to linger just a little too long on that person on the bus could be as 'pornographic' as sitting in a strip club.

You'll see this unfold through my own story and the real-world accounts of 13 brave women and men from all walks of life featured in this book (including my wife, best man, mum and pastor.)

What is an addiction?

There's a lot of debate about what people can be addicted to.

You may have heard people claim porn is just as addictive as cocaine, while others believe that's complete nonsense.

In a recent podcast interview with Tim Ferriss, Dr Gabor Maté gave the clearest description of an addiction I've ever heard.

He simply said for a habit to be defined as an addiction requires three things:

1. A short-term crave for pleasure
2. Negative long-term consequences
3. An inability to give it up

This is the definition I will be using.

Disclaimer: I'm not a doctor or mental health professional, and I don't claim to be. This book is not intended as a substitute for the advice of professional. Proceed at your own risk.

All I have is my story, and that's what I'm here to share.

I especially like the 3rd point, because many of us aren't aware we have an addiction until we actually try to give something up.

Porn is no different.

What about you?

When's the last time you've stopped for at least a month?

What's with all the spaces?

This book features very short paragraphs and lots of spaces, you will either love it or hate it, but here's a few reasons why:

1. Readability

This style of writing helps breaks the text up.

Not only does it make this book more accessible to people with short attention spans, but also for folk who don't like reading.

Plus it's more 'thumb-friendly' for people reading on a smart-phone and will read more like a blog post than a text-book.

2. Taking notes

I like to write and scribble over books. It helps me stay engaged and create action steps. Extra space helps.

We've also added a discussion section at the end of each chapter.

3. It's the way I write

Most of my writing is for the online world and I've just got in the habit of it. Sorry/you're welcome in advance.

P.S. If you hate it, get the audiobook for free via an Audible trial at https://matthewthompson.org/thebloodtippedblade/audiobook

(It's read by me and the people who share their stories in this book.)

Did you know...

"Porn sites receive more regular traffic than Netflix, Amazon, & Twitter combined each month" - Huffington Post

53% of boys and 39% of girls saw porn as a realistic depiction of sex." - BBC, 2016

"In 2013, the University of Montreal had to scrap planned research into the effects of pornography on society because they couldn't find any university aged males who hadn't been exposed to it."

According to NBC, the porn industry is worth over $97 billion.

"A generation of children are in danger of being stripped of their childhoods at a young age by stumbling across extreme and violent porn online." - NSPCC Chief Executive Peter Wanless, 2016

"56 percent of divorce cases involved one party having an obsessive interest in pornographic websites." - US Senate

"Over 40% of children ages 10 to 17 have been exposed to porn online, many accidentally. By college, according to a survey of more than 800 students titled 'Generation XXX,' 90% of men and one-third of women had viewed porn during the preceding year." - TIME Magazine

"Online pornography is severely corrupting today's youth: I see a sexual and relational train wreck happening..." - Dr. Aline Zoldbrod, Leading Sex Therapist

"Most pastors (57%) and youth pastors (64%) admit they have struggled with porn, either currently or in the past" - Barna

Plan Of Attack

For Steve, Nathan, Robin and Pete.

Thanks for fighting with me.

INTRO

Chapter 1 - The Tale of the Wolf

"Have you heard the fable of how people used to hunt wolves in the Arctic?"

I was 16 years old when I first heard this question, and the answer changed my relationship with pornography, lust and God forever.

The wolf is one of the deadliest predators known to man. Get in a cage with a wolf, and your chances of coming out again are pretty slim (unless you're Liam Neeson of course.)

Over the years, people got smart about how they hunted wolves, and as a result, they are extinct in many parts of the world today.

One hunting method in particular, has been a topic of curiosity and controversy...

Legend has it that Inuits - the people living in the Arctic - could take down a wolf with a single knife.

It goes something like this:

"Find a sharp knife and travel out to a part of the land you know is

wolf territory.

Cut yourself or an animal and smear the blood over the sharpest point.

Stick the weapon up in the ice and walk away.

The next morning you'll return to find a dead wolf."

But how?

"The wolf smells the blood a mile away and launches into hunt mode, coming in for the kill. Its adrenaline spikes, heart-rate quickens and eyes widen – ready for the chase ahead.

When the wolf arrives on the scene, it finds the blade. Perplexed it approaches the 'prey' with caution, sniffing and looking around as it does.

A little pool of blood resting at the base of the knife beckons the wolf to have a little taste...

Then; that rush and ravenous hunger kicks in.

The wolf slurps up the bloody slush around the knife before moving up to the blade itself. It can't stop. Besides, why would it want to when there seems to be an endless supply of blood coming its way?

Unaware that it is gorging on its own blood, the wolf continues feasting to satisfaction.

After some time the wolf feels tired.

It slows the consumption of the meal and decides to find somewhere to rest, but staggers and falls.

Confused, the wolf attempts to drag itself to refuge and shelter.

Each movement becomes slower and slower, and a trail of blood drags behind the wolf until it comes to a stop.

Its eyes slowly close over until they're finally shut, never to open again as the wolf would fail to make it through the night."

According to this fable, the Inuit's didn't need brute strength, lightning speed or even combat mastery.

They manipulated the hunger and instincts of the wolf to take down the prince of the Arctic with a single blood-tipped blade.

The first time I heard this little story, it put into pictures and words what I had been feeling for a long time. It confirmed the fears that deep down I knew were true but tried to ignore:

That porn was a blood-tipped blade in my life and I was the wolf falling into the hunter's trap.

Overkill? Perhaps, but the way I see it, lust is a blood-tipped blade in our culture today.

Millions of us have fallen into a trap thinking that what we are feeding on is giving us pleasure and satisfaction... when in the end it's actually hurting us.

I wrote this book from the perspective of a 23-year-old Christian living in Northern Ireland, but don't let that put you off if you come from a different faith, country or background.

This book is for people from all walks of life who know they have a problem and feel stuck.

This book is for those of you who are hungry for freedom and a new beginning.

This book is an invitation to see the other side of the story from someone who has 'been there, done that, clicked there, watched that.'

I by no means have all the answers, but I am willing to share my story - and the story of 13 others - along with what has helped us along the way.

I hope this book challenges and encourages you, no matter where you are on this incredible journey we call life.

- Matthew

THE HUNTERS

Chapter 2 - Who Are The Hunters?

"Wait there are hunters?!"

Well someone had to set the trap in the first place right?

Hunters can come in many shapes and forms, but they all have the same goal: **to keep us stuck in a cycle of addiction.**

If you've ever tried to make a significant change in your life then you know it can often feel like the whole world is against you.

How there seems to be a criminal mastermind plan to catch you out…

This doesn't just happen with porn, but pretty much every area of our lives.

Here's a real-life example.

Windowsill Cigarettes

When I was 18 years old, I left Northern Ireland to go and work for a non-profit in NYC for 3 years.

We worked with loads of incredible people from Manhattan's homeless community, some of whom battled drug and alcohol addictions.

Unlike pornography addictions, these issues are often very visual, allowing you to see very clearly the journey to freedom, or the relapse away from it.

The CEO of the non-profit (to whom much of this book is indebted to) worked at a rehabilitation program in Los Angeles before living in NYC.

They ran a really tight program out in LA. Once you signed up, you had to cut out **everything** you were taking, including booze, drugs and *even cigarettes.*

If you took any of these substances while in the program you would either have to start all over again or leave.

There's a curious story my boss would always tell that has stuck with me to this day.

Basically, there was a man who was getting on really well in the program.

He was on track and making incredible progress in overcoming his addictions. But, one day while out doing community work in the city he had a 'chance' encounter.

To his surprise, someone had a left a full packet of cigarettes and a lighter sitting on a windowsill.

He glanced around to see if anyone was looking before helping himself to 'just one cigarette.' 3 days later he was back on the streets in over his head in heavy drugs again.

This small trigger of a smoking a cigarette led to a downward spiral with devastating consequences.

He reverted back to his previous behaviour and way of life.

Now, it can be easy for us to pass judgement or sympathy here, but perhaps this is more relevant than we initially think.

In NYC I saw this happen time and time again on the streets, but I've also seen it in shiny church pews, flashy corporate offices and in my own life.

How often have we decided just to bend one of our rules just a little bit only to end up in over our own heads and back where we started?

"Just one more time."
"This is the last one."
"I'm going to stop next week."

We've all been there.

But that's not the point of the story. The point of the story is to ask some questions for us to think about.

Who put the cigarettes there?

Was it just an unlucky situation or was it intentional?

Why did he smoke the cigarettes?

Who is making money off this man's addiction?

The Donut Dilemma

Here's a less severe and perhaps more relatable scenario.

(Side note: apparently, this book is subliminally sponsored by donuts so apologies for all the references in advanced. Belfast - our capital city - has gone absolutely donut-crazy recently, so they're on my mind a lot and have become a recurring theme in the book, but I'm just going to run with it.)

We've all been there.

Committed to finally getting that beach bod, Googled a pro-gram, set our alarms early for the gym and got our healthy meals prepped for the day.

But something unusual happens. Something out of the ordinary. For the first time in history, our work/school/granny decides to buy donuts for everyone.

"Would you like one? I picked out the chocolate glazed one just for you?"

All of a sudden everyone wants to buy us the unhealthy food we love, at the very moment we've decided to give it up.

Unbelievable.

What gives?

For those of you who have ever stepped out and tried to stand against something or make a change in your life - you know that the opposition you face is not only huge, but often very personal.

Almost… strategic.

Many write this off as bad luck, but some of us are starting to think that these 'chances' are too perfectly planned, due to their timing (usually in our weakest moments) and their nature (often something we can't refuse, like free donuts in the office the day we start a diet.)

Not to get all hocus pocus on you, but I believe this is the work of **THE HUNTERS**: *the antagonists that every great story must have in order to be great.*

We all face many types of hunters in our lives, but I'd like to talk about what I consider 'the big 3.'

Be warned: #3 may come as a surprise.

Hunter #1: The Porn Industry

We live in an age overloaded by content, information and art for us to consume at any moments notice.
Most of us do this digitally, and the average person can spend up to 4 hours a day doing so.

The strange thing is that 99% of it is free.

Have you ever stopped to think about how weird that it?

After all, even most porn is free.

How can this be when somebody had to make this content?

The cost of free

For the last 2 years, I've worked in advertising as a freelance copy-writer

(I'm the guy who writes the text on websites, blogs and ads.)

It's a lot of fun, extremely interesting and a great opportunity for me to develop my craft as a writer and skills as a marketer.

We live in an age where advertising and content marketing is a powerful force, and as good ole Uncle Ben says *"with great power comes great responsibility."*

Unfortunately, that responsibility often gets mistreated.

In my opinion, all the recent scandals surrounding Facebook, user data and advertising is just the tip of an iceberg that goes deeper than we can possibly imagine.

We advertisers/marketers have access to an insane amount of personal data and tools to try and leverage everything we can to make you do what we want.

(And we're often prepared to spend a huge amount of money, time and talent to make that happen.)

This is a true but hard statement to accept: nothing in life is free.

No one on the planet truly works for free because all work demands something in return.

Even if it just a smile, a thank you or a few seconds of someone's precious attention there is always a transaction taking place.

For example, some of you may have received this book for free, but you're still spending precious time to read it *(up to this point anyway.)*

I'm not saying we all need to become hyper-skeptical, but an awareness that 'free' isn't 'free' is helpful.

Espcially online.

For example, the porn industry is one of the most lucrative and influential industries out there, yet the majority of its content is free to access.

(Same with YouTube.)

They know that by hooking us in with free content, they can lead us down carefully designed funnels (user journeys) to get us to part with our cash, while also making money with every click/tap we make via ads.

But of course, we pay much more than merely our time or money as this book will show or as you already know.

We pay a high price, personally, emotionally, physically and perhaps even spiritually.

In the darkest moments of my addiction, I like the wolf, discovered there really is *no such thing as a free lunch.*

Perhaps you can relate too.

Hunter #2: The Enemy (Optional)

Also referred to as the devil, satan, Lucifer or 'the father of lies', the enemy is Christianity's antagonist featured throughout the Bible, from the serpent in Genesis, to the dragon in Revelation.

Naturally, some of you will think this is the biggest pile of *insert colourful word of your choice.*

That's fine.

I realise our opinions/beliefs may split here (if they haven't already.)

If it triggers you so much, go ahead and skip to the 3rd hunter.

Who is he?

Many people much smarter than I are divided over the nitty gritty details of who he is and where he came from, so for the purposes of this book, we will avoid diving deep into them.

The general consensus is that the enemy tried to lead a rebellion against God at the age of time, lost miserable and was banished to roam the earth until the end of time.

A few thousand years after Adam and Eve listened to the serpent and rebelled against God, the enemy is still up to his old tactics of spreading lies, fear and chaos.

Peter, the fisherman-disciple extraordinaire and one of Jesus' BFFs had this to say about the enemy.

"Stay alert! Watch out for your great enemy the devil. He prowls around like a roaring lion, looking for someone to devour." - 1 Peter 5:8

Generally speaking, I have a real problem with how much power the church attributes to 'the devil.'

It bothers me when people blame the devil for making them late even though in reality they just didn't get up in time...

I think very often we blame the enemy for things we're responsible for and give him credit (or is it discredit?) to things he had nothing to do with (more on this later.)

But, Peter's words are an important warning to us all.

For those of you who don't know, Peter was a pretty brave guy...

His montage moments include: walking on water, slashing some-one's ear off with a sword, leading the early church movement and getting crucified upside down.

Plus he was a fisherman who faced the ACTUAL storms of life on a regular basis.

So when he says 'hey be careful, don't take this threat lightly' I can't help but listen.

Then you have the fact that Ephesians 6:12 reminds us we're caught up in the middle of a spiritual battle, that there's always more going on behind the scenes then we perhaps intially think...

"For we are not fighting against flesh-and-blood enemies, but against evil rulers and authorities of the unseen world, against mighty powers in this dark world, and against evil spirits in the heavenly places."

This gets me fired up.

It adds purpose and meaning to my life knowing that each day I'm taking part in this epic war between good and evil.

However, like any battle, there are serious risks, dangers and con-sequences involved.

But there are also incredible opportunities for victory.

It all depends on how you fight, why you fight, who you fight for and who you fight with.

Hunter #3: Ourselves

Plot twist.

Here's the deal: The last thing I want you to take from this book is "oh Matthew says the devil and the porn industry are the reason why I'm addicted to porn and I'm no match against forces that strong."

Nope.

That's not the case. I'm not saying that the devil is hiding under your bed trying to get you to watch porn every night, or that the industry sits down to discuss how they can get 10 year olds addicted to their products.

These forces merely create the opportunity. At the end of the day it's us who take them.

You see, we all love someone to blame.

It abdicates us of any responsibility, control or ability to change our situation. It's the easy way out.

But we don't want that way any more, because victims are not victors.

It's far easier to blame big corporations or the bogeyman for our problems than it is to look in the mirror and accept that we have a choice and a role to play.
Here are a few examples from the pens of history.

"It's not what happens to you, but how you react to it that matters." - Epictetus (Greek stoic.)

"When we can no longer change a situation, we are challenged to change ourselves." - Viktor Frankl (Holocaust survivor.)

"I don't control life, but I can control how I react to it" - Macklemore (former drug-addict and world-famous musician)

In the first few drafts of this book, I exclusively focused on how outside forces were to blame for our problem and this epidemic.

But this isn't the full picture.

The reality is we often become our own hunters.

We self-sabotage ourselves and make choices that set us up for failure, both consciously and unconsciously. Internal forces often fight against us, pulling us away from a full and noteworthy life.

One of the greatest biblical heroes - the Apostle Paul - actually wrote about this exact point explicitly in Romans 7:18-19.

"I want to do what is right, but I can't. I want to do what is good, but I don't. I don't want to do what is wrong, but I do it anyway."

The Hunter Within

This inner hunter has been referred to as many things over the years.

- Stephen Pressfield calls it 'The Resistance' in The Art Of War.
- Seth Godin labels it as 'The Lizard Brain' in Linchpin.
- The Bible refers to it as 'our sinful nature' or 'the flesh.'

Acknowledging these internal hunters is key so we can wage war against them because in my experience they are the toughest to beat.

Besides,

Few of us will actually go up head to head with the porn industry.

Few of us will have a showdown with the devil in the wilderness.

But all of us must face the hunter in the mirror.

In the next chapter we're going to take a look at why these hunters hunt.

Acknowledging who we're fighting against and how they do it is essential to grasp before diving into the tools, mindsets and steps we can take to beat them.

But first, we must start with why.

Why do the hunters hunt?

STORIES FROM THE WOLFPACK
- Anghell Sanchez: Former Sex Addict

Who are you?

Interesting question, not quite sure how to answer it, probably because I am still trying to figure that out! My name is Anghell Sanchez, a woman just a few weeks shy of her 30th birthday.

Professionally, I've been a student, an intern, a therapist, a waitress and a director in a city ministry.

Personally, I'm a daughter, the oldest of 3, a sister, a roommate, a friend, a godmother and someone who passionately loves Jesus (a Christian.)

I am wild at heart, rebellious, adventurous, stubborn and very hard on myself, but very loving to others.

I am also a woman who has battled with compulsive sex, porn and masturbation to different extents and periods of my life since December of 2007.

Is lust just a guy's issue?

Ha! Seriously?! Do people honestly still believe that? Absolutely not!

I first discovered porn on accident when I was 8 or 9. My childhood neighbour and I were playing in the backyard area of our apartment complex and next to the laundry room was the trash and peering out of the silver can was a shiny adult magazine.

Even as a child I vividly recall being so aroused, a new feeling for me.

Around 10 or 11 I remember masturbating. I had no idea what I was doing or most importantly why, all I knew was that it felt good.

Oddly enough for the next few years of my life all of that stuff was completely taken out of my life.

The only explanation I have is that I was filling that void with drugs- weed, ecstasy, shrooms, alcohol and self-harm. As a teen, I was hanging with the wrong crowd and associating with my neighbourhood gang (mostly for protection.)

The girls around me started getting pregnant and having to drop out of school.

Witnessing that at 13/14 changed my perspective. I was ok with the recreational drink and drug use but I was definitely not going to engage in sexual activity.

After all, I couldn't end up like them and get stuck in my hometown forever.

I felt a little superior for not getting pregnant while it seemed everyone around me was.

In December 2007 that all changed.

I was 17 and by that stage I had already kissed boys, and fooled around with them but nothing too explicit yet.

Once I began having sex, it became a daily occurrence. I presently know that I am hypersexual but in retrospect I recognise I've always been that way.

It got to the point I was skipping college so much so that they warned me that I wouldn't obtain my associate's degree and transfer on time if something didn't change.

All of this was happening while I was trying to figure out my faith, and trying to be obedient to God's word (a contradiction you may say, but this was my reality.)

I moved away for my undergrad and decided that a new city would be the perfect place to start afresh. I decided I would get my life together, stop engaging in risky sexual activity and that I was determined to exercise celibacy.

I had no idea how challenging that would be and I didn't know the many other dark doors that struggle would open including meeting up with strangers from online hook-up websites.

During the next 4 years, I lost track of how many online strangers I met up with in person.

The dangers of online encounters never fully dawned on me and I am grateful I was not murdered and found in an abandoned car trunk.

However, the reality of this possibility never deterred me from continuing to engage in such risky behaviour.

How does lust compare to a drug addiction? Are you sure you can REALLY get addicted to stuff like this?

Absolutely.

I finally decided to get help.

THE HUNTERS

I started attending SCA meetings, 12 step meetings for those struggling with sexually compulsive behaviour.

The irony of learning about these meetings is that I learned about their existence while obtaining my certification in counselling and was about to enter the workforce as a substance abuse therapist!

During my first two internships in the field people wondered why I had such an uncanny ability to relate to addicts or alcoholics. They didn't know it was because I was an addict myself.

In my training, I learned all about addiction, the pleasure path of the brain and how powerful the memory of the nucleus accumbens can be.

I learned the concept of always chasing the initial high left the regions of the brain forever affected and creates a pre-disposition to alcoholism and drug addiction.

In my professional opinion, you can 100% become addicted to sex, porn, masturbation etc because like drugs and alcohol those behaviours all go through the same pleasure path.

As an addict, there are times when you get a real wake-up call. Something that very tangibly shows you just how far you've fallen or how much damage is really being done.

For me it was a positive diagnosis of HSV-2 (herpes.)

I was also informed I was HPV positive and had the two strands that cause cervical cancer and could potentially leave me sterile.

This jolted me to stop… For a while.

The changes I made were only exterior and in the depths of my soul I was no different to a heroin addict who starts misusing methadone (a drug used to help people get off heroin) instead of actually shooting up the real stuff.

I stopped sleeping around and instead began dabbling in the cyber world of pornography and masturbation.

I had exchanged one dangerous behaviour for another.

People will argue that porn and masturbation do not have any adverse effects and that it's actually is healthy/necessary.

I scoff at that ignorant statement because in my eyes nothing could be further from the truth.

While my new "healthier" habit was slowly getting out of control, I found myself having sex again, except, this time it looked very similar to the kind of videos I had been watching.

I began engaging in some truly outrageous, dangerous, and degrading encounters.

I had trained my brain to enjoy these activities and to only achieve pleasure through such extreme measures.

What would you say to encourage the 16 year old version of yourself?

My parents never talked to me about sex (taboo in Latino culture I guess).

The only thing my dad ever told me was "you're worth more than what you have between your legs."

When I tried asking what he meant he abruptly and nervously

changed the subject and never brought it up again.

If I could go back to my 17-year-old self that festive December night I would advise her to exercise self-love and convince her that love and sex are not interchangeable.

It might be too late for my 17-year-old self, but it's not too late for you and it's not too late for my 30-year-old self.

After all, we're all on a journey and must cling to the hope that freedom is indeed possible.

Side Note: I feel that sexual addictions are so much complicated and strenuous to break because physical substances (like drugs) are foreign to our bodies and don't naturally belong to our human nature and creation.

Our sexual desire however, is part of our humanity.
So when battling sexual addiction we are in part fighting our human nature.

Our current culture has a lot to say about our "sexual liberation," but it's all lies.

Sex within the healthy context of a God-ordained marriage is beautiful and the way it was meant to be.

Battling between culture and God's way can often seem impossible, but it is the only way we can overcome these compulsive behaviours.

— *Anghell Sanchez*

Discussion Questions

1. How did the story of the wolf make you feel? Could you relate in any way?

2. Why do you think we do certain things even though we know they have negative outcomes?

3. What are the 'blood tipped blades' in your life? Is it porn? Social media? Something else?

4. What was your biggest takeaway from Anghell's story?

Chapter 3 - Why do the hunters hunt?

"Ok so why are they going after me?!"

Good question. While I haven't personally interviewed everyone involved, I'd like to put forward a few suggestions.

Let's take a look at the motivation behind the big 3.

Hunter #1: The Porn Industry

So, it's tempting to dive in straight away and say that it's money.

After all, the porn industry is a business, and one of the most profitable ones around.

But I would argue that the driving motivation behind the industry is not merely money, but rather **humanity.**

That sounds quite profound, but I promise you it's not.

When I say humanity I'm talking about our human desires for corruptible things like money, power, wealth, status, fame and success all the way to wholesome things like love, respect and connection.

It's a combination of the above that drives most people in general, and the people behind the porn industry are no different.

These are real-life men and women just like you and me.

They have hopes, fears and dreams just like us.

Don't make the mistake that so many people in the anti-porn movement make in dehumanising those involved, whether it's the tech geek in the office, young woman operating the camera or the male porn star on the other side of the lens.

Please note: this doesn't abdicate them of responsibility, they obviously have a monumental role to play in all of this, but I do want to challenge our views about those involved.

They have fallen for their own blood-tipped blade laid out by the hunters they face in their own lives.

Really when you strip it back, they are no different to you or me.

Hunter #2: The Enemy (optional)

Again, I'm not a theologian and won't pretend to be, so we'll keep this section fairly brief.

Here are a few suggestions of why I think the enemy hunts us.

1. He is immensely jealous

When God made human beings he made us very different to everything else in the universe.

You see we are the only things in the universe made in God's image.

All that creativity, desire to build, emotional depth and passion are only found in one part of creation...

You.

Me.

Us.

God loves you and loves me more than anything else he has ever made. We are God's masterpiece, the crown of creation, his beloved.

Is it possible that the devil is immensely jealous of this?

That God could love and put something as weak, small and feeble as us above the hunter?

While I haven't personally met him, I do get the vibe that he hates not being number 1...

2. Revenge

Think throughout history, recent and afar.

If you want to take revenge on someone, you have two options: Attack them personally or attack the things they care about most.

Usually, that means attacking the people your opposition cares about the most. As a result, family and friends are often targeted and abused as a way of revenge.

History is also full of occasions where family members 'defect' to the other side.

Princes join the rebels to fight against their parents and kids go to work for the big competitor of the family business.

This betrayal hurts.

The enemy knows that dragging us away from God is a great way to carry out his revenge.

Like any good father, it pains God so much to see his children suffering and hurting.

Could this be a reason why this hunter hunts?

3. Misery loves company

As already mentioned, the devil is on a deadline.

He knows his time is running out, so even though victory isn't achievable, he has committed himself to cause as much damage as possible before he goes out.

To 'drag all of us down with him' for lack of a better term.

You see God has amazing things planned for our lives (and this whole planet,) but he can't force it to happen.

The responsibility and choice lies with us.

So, the enemy tries his best to pull us away from walking in God's plans, and he will stop at nothing to try and derail us from these things.

Hunter #3: Ourselves

Our internal forces often wage war against our true passions, callings or desires.

Again, as Paul said:

"I want to do what is right, but I can't. I want to do what is good, but I don't. I don't want to do what is wrong, but I do it anyway." - Romans 7:18-19

There has been A LOT of great writing about this, but in short, I believe we do this out of fear.

- Fear that we'll fail.
- Fear that we'll succeed.
- Fear that we'll have no more excuses holding us back.

A porn addiction can be a great excuse for:

- Why our marriages/relationships aren't working out.
- Why we're not pursuing a leadership role in our church or organisation.
- Why we're not creating the amazing art we were born to create.

We can subconsciously use our addictions as a form of self-sabotage due to these fears or consciously use them to numb pain, escape reality and/or cope with a difficult situation/relationship.

All addiction is rooted in some form of pain. To deal with this pain, we turn to things like drugs, alcohol, porn, sex, video games or social media.

None of these things are bad in themselves, it's when they become excessive and outside of our control that things can get messy.

It's important to ask yourself some key questions at this stage.

"Why do I watch porn?"

"What pain am I self-medicating against?"

Is it loneliness? Isolation? Depression?

Do I even know?

One of the best ways to deal with a porn addiction is to deal with the reason WHY you use porn in the first place.

I'm talking about beyond the surface level "because it feels good" and so on.

You need to dig deep here and uncover your why.

For me, it was to escape my reality.

My health was poor and things at home were difficult. I chose to escape into a virtual reality of gaming and pornography because I didn't want to deal with my true reality.

I chose to escape, to check-out. The problem was when my situation improved, I was still engaged and stuck in my old habits.

That was the point I realised I was addicted.

Like many people, I only really knew I had a problem whenever I tried to stop and couldn't, despite years of desperately trying on my own.

I was around 14/15.

What about you?

Why does this continue to be an issue in your life?

What pain are you trying to numb or reality are you trying to escape from?

This book won't answer these questions for you because only you can answer them.

A way to do this is by engaging in the discussion questions at the end of each chapter and actually taking the time to complete them.

It is essential to take time to explore yourself and the root of your addiction. Seek therapy/counselling if you have the opportunity to do so because my experience/story will only take you so far.

At the end of the day, you are the one who has to take action.

Merely reading a book isn't going to change anything.

I know it feels like our bodies are fighting against us, but that's often just the way it is.

Our flesh loves the short-term. In fact, it's all it cares about.

Eating, sleeping, protecting and reproducing.

Nothing else matters to the body beyond survival and pleasure.

But the thing is, we weren't just born to survive.

We were born to thrive.

"Ok so how does this relate to my porn problem?"

I believe the industry profits off young men and women becoming addicted to their sites and products they sell.

I believe the enemy is using pornography as a full frontal assault against the youth of today because we are the future of tomorrow and have the power/potential to turn the world around.

I believe that many of us use pornography as a means to escape our reality instead of rising up to our full potential.

And I believe all of these hunters have crafted a clever, multi-layered strategy to stop us in our tracks and prevent us becoming the world changers we were made to be.

In the next chapter, we're going to look at *how* they do this.

STORIES FROM THE WOLFPACK
- Ross Robinson: Never an Addict

Who are you?

My name is Ross Robinson; I'm a 23 year old dental student graduating this summer.

I love to exercise, catch up with friends over a good coffee and after a few years of trying I'm actually starting to enjoy reading!

What has been your experience with porn?

My first experience of porn was at 12 years old on the school bus with my friends, coming home from a Saturday rugby match.

A group of lads started forming at the back of the bus, and by their reaction, everyone knew something exciting and mischievous was going down.

"Ross, come here and see this."

I didn't want to come across as the 'good kid,' so I walked to the back of the bus and watched the video.

My mind couldn't even fathom what I was looking at.

I only watched porn once more after that, more so out of curiosity.

One evening, just before going to bed, I decided to get my laptop out and go to a website I heard some of my friends talking about.

I watched a video for about 20 seconds but to be honest, although it sounds cliche, I felt so 'dirty.'

Quickly closing the tab, I deleted my search history just in case my parents came looking...

I swore to myself that I'd never watch it again and it's a blessing that I never did.

How did that make you feel?

Even though I never developed an addiction to porn, the cultural impact still affected me.

During the early years of secondary school, I felt weird and isolated because I was the only one not consuming.

I knew I fancied girls, but the fact that I didn't participate in watching porn with the lads or masturbate several times a day like everyone else led me to have loads of questions.

"Why am I so different to the other guys?"
"What's wrong with me?"
"Am I gay?"

Looking back now it's crazy to think that my story was the exception to the rule.

Matthew actually even said that I'm the first guy his age he's ever met who wasn't addicted to porn at some point in their life.

(I guess that's why I made it into the book!)

What advice would you give to someone who doesn't struggle with porn?

Not struggling with porn is a blessing and something to be very thankful for.

I know hundreds of people who wish that was the case for them.

Even though it may seem like everyone around you is doing it, I can assure you that you're not missing out.

There is nothing wrong with you.

You are perfectly normal.

In fact, you are highly blessed!

On the other hand, it's important to show grace and compassion to people in your life who do have a problem with porn.

Don't put yourself above them… even secretly in your mind.

There may also be a temptation "to test how strong you really are."

This is dangerous territory.

As they say… if you play with fire, you will eventually get burnt.

So why bother risking it? It's simply just not worth it.

I assume just because you didn't have a porn problem doesn't mean you've lived a flawless, easy life?

Haha. Of course not.

The reality is of course that just because you don't struggle with porn, doesn't mean you aren't susceptible to struggling with other things that can destroy your mind!

I personally struggled for a number of years with my body image - how I looked - and that led me to becoming 'addicted' to the gym.

Missing one day at the gym was like a disaster to me. Not being known as

the 'lanky tall' guy consumed my mind and became all I cared about.

Thankfully I've walked on a journey to overcome that and establish a healthy relationship with myself and exercise, which is now a real source of joy in my life.

What's one thing that has helped you overcome the battle in your mind?

There's one analogy that has helped me over the years.

Basically, 2000+ years ago, cities had tall walls around them to protect them from the enemies attack and the only way you could get in was through the city gates.

If the gates weren't locked or well guarded, the enemies could storm the city and destroy everything/everyone inside and take control.

Our eyes are like the gates to our mind.

If we aren't careful of what we see or look at with our eyes, we too could be susceptible to 'attack', allowing our mind to be 'destroyed' and the for the 'enemy' to seize control…

Whatever that enemy is.

I've discovered endless amounts of practical wisdom a simple lyric from a kid's Sunday School song…

"Oh be careful little eyes what you see."

Discussion questions

1. When is the last time you haven't watched porn for at least one month?

2. What pain do you think is at the root of your porn consumption?

3. In what ways have you potentially self-sabotaged yourself in the last month?

4. What's your biggest takeaway from Ross' story?

Chapter 4 - How Do The Hunters Hunt?

"The enemy comes to seek, kill and destroy..." - John 10:10

John 10:10 has been the most important bit of the Bible for me in my life so far.

This is the first half (I'll talk about the rest later) and I think it's probably the closest thing to a mission statement of the enemy you'll find.

In this chapter, we'll break it down and put it into the context of pornography and our 3 hunters.

I'll also walk you through some of my own story and journey along the way.

Let's do it.

1. Seek

While hunters don't mind a fight, like most predators they will the choose the easy option and prey on the weak/vulnerable if they get the opportunity.

The path of least resistance so to speak.

We see this played out in the average age of exposure to porn which is often cited between 10-13 years old.

Based on hundreds of conversations with people from all over the world I know that number to be true.

Pornography found us all in different ways. Some of us through older siblings, a friends sleepover or in the case of a good friend of mine, through their dad.

But, I would say the biggest way is of course through the internet and specifically, through carefully designed click funnels and user journeys.

Like cubs in the den or chicks in the nest, we simply didn't stand a chance against such a cunning and devious opponent.

It's actually shocking how few clicks it takes to get to porn from even the most reputable and well-known websites out there.

Banner ads and "suggested articles" are often a smooth slippery slope to sexual content.

Another tactic is to leak/distribute softcore content across channels like YouTube, Facebook and other social media platforms with links to take you to the 'full version.'

You may be surprised at just how explicit content can be on websites like Instagram, Pinterest and Tumblr if you go looking for it.

But then again, a lot of you know exactly what I'm talking about.

As a child, it's a relatively fast grooming process fueled by our own curiosity.

From the soft stuff, we make our ways onto XXX hardcore websites that have thousands of free, long-form content hidden behind a simple box anyone can tick to say they are over the age of 18.

A cycle of masturbation and self-gratification usually follows (though we don't need any external help to figure that one out.)

The sad thing is that most of us had no one to warn us or protect us.

Parents, teachers and other guardians in our lives failed to keep us safe from the world of streamable porn because they were trying to figure out the internet for themselves (or at least the latest advancements of it.)

Things moved so fast for my parent's generation that it was impossible for anyone to keep up.

I remember my first exposure to something explicit online.

I was 10 years old.

It happened while searching for a Super Mario poster for my room on a well-known website (yes I was a geek.)

I couldn't find what I was looking for, so I began to browse.

A recommended poster popped up for sale with a photo of a well-known model I had seen on T.V.

Only this time she was naked.

My 10-year-old jaw hit the desk in my wee boyhood room. I

stared on for a few minutes in horror, amazement, disgust and arousal.

When my foster brother stormed into the room unannounced I swiftly shut the computer down and vowed to myself 'never to do that again.'

Of course, I did.

A curiosity had awoken in me that I couldn't shrug.

From there I turned to MTV music videos, softcore stuff on You-Tube and then ultimately to full-blown porn on the most well-known site that was just a quick Google away.

I remember getting the first generation of an iPod touch (similar to an iPhone) the year it came out.

The thing didn't even have apps on it yet.

In a few short years, I could stream HD porn on it any time, any place I wanted straight from the porn-provider's apps.

A deadly progression took place in a short space of time.

At each step, I consumed more and more extreme content.

At each step, I felt the same disgust as the first time but had to go even further the next time to get the same rush.

I think many of us actually get hooked to this rush and therefore end up going places we could never have imagined all while feeling immense shame along the way.

In her fantastic TED Talk, Dr Gail Hines conveys this brilliantly.

Here's a brief excerpt about her discussing the journey of the average 12-year-old watching the extremely abusive content found in mainstream porn.

He's 12-years-old, he's going into manhood, he's aroused. [The pornographers] are telling him:

"You wanna be a male?"
"This is your entree into masculinity."
"This is the price you pay to be masculine."

And in that boy's stomach is a toxic stew, because he's aroused, but he's also ashamed, and he's also scared, and he's also angry, and he feels enormous shame because he feels aroused and nobody has said to him:

"This is not who you are" because the pornographers say to him: "This is who you are. This is what you want"

By the age of 13, there was virtually nothing I hadn't seen.

The hunters had sought me out, and I was hooked.

2. Kill

What a lot of people don't realise is that the porn industry as we know it has been primarily scaled by techies, not porn stars or directors.

People who can code. People who can design websites. People who can analyse data.

I highly recommend listening to Jon Ronson's incredible podcast series The Butterfly Effect on Audible or Apple Podcasts.

In it, Ronson and the team dive deep into the origins of the modern porn industry and the people behind it.

I think it does a fantastic job of investigating how we got here while also doing a beautiful job of sharing the humanity of everyone involved.

The temptation is to view the people involved in a very negative light, but as mentioned they are just as human as you and me and got into the industry in a wide range of ways and all for different reasons.

They have very kindly allowed me to share some excerpts with you in this book.

One interview was with a gentleman called Brendan.

Brendan is a talented techie with a speciality in mobile-technology.

He was headhunted to work for a company who in 2012 controlled around 80% of online porn.

In the interview, he shared how they would optimise each webpage to encourage people to click through and spend time on the site.

Check it out:

"We send different versions to different people... [We] can determine if we use Version A we'll see 10% more clicks, so we then send Version A to the entire population. Then we do another A/B test until you test and test and test until you reach a point where you know we're not going to get any better than this."

Now, this isn't shocking considering just about every major website out there uses this technique.

It involves changing images, text and layout to see what gets the best results.

Brendan describes the company as being similar to Facebook or Google. Ordinary-looking offices with people working on computers.

You see, a large percentage of porn is filmed in California while offices such as Brendan's are located thousands of miles away...

For Brendan, it was never about porn for him. He never visited the filming sets, and he never was involved in the creation of the content.

"All I saw was modules, advertisements and dollar signs."

His job was merely to optimise the websites containing the content and get as many people to see it as possible.

I mention this for two reasons.

1. To show you how the people involved are human.
2. To show you just how smart and strategic the industry is.

An immense amount of effort goes into ensuring that the blood-tipped blade (the bait/trap) is as desirable as possible.

Combine that with our natural curiosity and sex drive and are we really surprised that so many people fall into the porn-trap?

Obviously, I'm anti-porn in general because, but what really infuriates me is how easily accessible porn is for minors (kids.)

In my opinion and in my experience, early exposure to porn is a recipe for disaster.

THE HUNTERS

When exposed at a young age, our minds aren't ready to process what our eyes are seeing (in fact, most of us watched porn before our bodies were even physically ready for sex.)

Our innocence and purity were slaughtered. Stolen away from us before the right time.

This adds a whole new sombre spin on the often-quoted Song Of Songs verse: *don't awaken love until the time is right.* (8:4)

It's a devasting death to any childhood because it changes the way a child looks at the world.

How they look at adults, peers and the people they end up becoming attracted to.

I know it did for me anyway.

Writing from a heterosexual males perspective, women became objects of self-gratification. Something to be looked at, consumed and then thrown away as quickly as you could delete your browsing history.

I found it harder to have innocent relationships with the girls in my class because I had spent the night before in a digital fantasy that corrupted my reality.

Besides, adding pornography to the diet of a hormone packed teenager is like throwing petrol on a fire.

When the miraculous happened, and some poor girl agreed to date my goofy, spotty, insecure self, I had no idea how to actually love or care for someone in a relationship.

Plus, things got physical so quickly that it almost seemed unavoidable.

Can you relate to that?

The sad thing is that our high-school sweethearts usually just went with it because they were on the same pornified track we were on.

Then just like our private digital habits, we rinsed and repeated, moved onto another girl/guy just like we moved onto another website to start the process again.

Sound familiar?

This is the experience of most people my age. In fact, I've only ever met one male my age who has never been addicted to porn and it was Ross, from the end of the last chapter.

Even writing this now I can only think of one word.

Heartbreaking.

My friends and I look back on our teenage years fondly, but also aware of the hurt and pain we caused to others and experienced ourselves because of our porn problems.

We are more than aware of how we played in the hunters' traps and became hunters ourselves.

Aware of how a certain part of our innocence/childhood was killed off at an early age and that we weren't able to get it back.

(This is doom and gloom stuff I know! But bear with me. We gotta start here before moving forward. There's one last bit of the hunter equation to go then it's time to move onto THE WOLF section.)

3. Destroy

The story of the wolf differs from reality in one crucial way…

Once the wolf is dead, the story is over.

However, for us, we wake up in the morning and are launched back into the same scenario every single day like some sort of weird groundhog day.

Baited, trapped, killed. Repeat.
Baited, trapped, killed. Repeat.

It's like one of those movies that repeat the same day over and over again.

When you're a porn addict, it's easy to feel like a wolf destined to chase it's own tail forever.´

In my eyes, this is the most brutal aspect of the hunters' tactics - to keep us trapped in a cycle.

It's also extremely profitable for the industry because they get to create customers for life.

Here's another quote from Brendan about how the monetisation strategy works for free porn sites:

"What we would do is use the [free] sites to promote paid content… you have this kind of washing machine effect where the whole company is doing well because the [free] sites are promoting the paid site content and also selling ads."

Where addiction comes into this is open for debate and I think requires a lot more research.
But I know myself and others have found the following to be true:

- **Physiologically:** we can get hooked on the reaction our brain has to porn in ways not so radically different to drugs.

- **Behaviorally:** we start to use porn/masturbation/hookups as coping mechanisms for rough days, exam stress or problems at home.

- **Emotionally:** we use lust as a way to escape our reality and get lost in a fantasy world where we can run away to, even if it's just for a few seconds.

It's the same reason why we get drunk, take drugs, play video games, read books or eat a box of donuts.

We all have 'our thing' to distract ourselves instead of dealing with the real problems life throws our way.

You'll notice I haven't explicitly focused on 'the devil' or 'ourselves' in this chapter. That's because those two hunters are interwoven into every piece of the puzzle and the lines are often blurred.

We deal with blurred lines in general when it comes to issues of lust because they touch on something so close to who we are as people.

'The drug' as such is mingled with our natural sex-drives and appetites.

The masturbation addict's drug is with them at all times because it's part of their own body.

The thing about alcohol and a drug like cocaine is that it causes very tangible and visibly destructive results. Often you can tell someone is an addict just from their physical appearance.

Sadly people lose their jobs, marriages, get sick and even die.

But porn has a less visible impact. On the surface, we look fine.

But behind the church smile, locked doors and deleted search history, lies an ugly and destructive force.

A force that ruins lives, destroys marriages and bankrupts a person's self-confidence/perception of reality.

The sad thing is most of us have never told anyone, so we face it alone in silence.

I was 16 the first time I ever mentioned to someone what I was going through.

That was 5 years of isolation in some of the most formative and difficult years of my life.

Honestly, this is why I'm writing this book, because I don't want this to be true for anyone else.

The cultural taboo and heavy stigma stop us from opening our mouths and speaking out. The enemy uses shame and guilt to keep us quiet, an age-old tactic that has worked since the Garden of Eden.

"What would your parents think?!"

"What will your friends say?!"

"They don't struggle with this stuff."

"You're a freak, and you're alone in this struggle."

Deadly whispers that hold us down.

But not for long.

This book is a megaphone to call out things the way they are.

To shout about the industries that target and prey on young people to trap us in a cycle and make money from our struggle.
To scream against the lies that tell you that you're all alone, that no one else struggles with this and that there is no way out.

I'm putting myself on the line for you guys.

I'm letting the whole world that my name is Matthew Thompson and I was addicted to pornography from 11 to 16 years old because I don't want you to have to walk the road I had to.

It's time to end this taboo.

No 11 year old should have to stay silent about stuff like this.

I now have the pleasure of saying I was addicted (past tense) because thanks to an awesome Wolfpack of friends, the tactics I'm going to share in 'THE ALPHA' section and a lot of fight I was set free.

But before jumping into the practical steps you can take, it's essential that we take a closer look at ourselves and the world that we live in.

It's vital that we know the way things were supposed to be before we try and change our environments, communities and cultures.

Let's do it and let's do it together.

STORIES FROM THE WOLFPACK
- Nils Arnell: Confessions of a Church-Kid

My name is Nils Arnell, and I was addicted to pornography for more than a decade.

It all started around the time I was eleven years old when I hit puberty. It was also at that time I realised I was different than my friends.

Unlike my friends, who were all interested in girls, I was attracted to guys.

Everyone's story is different, and for me, the addiction started small.

Among other things, the men's underwear section in clothing magazines got my attention and as time went by that turned into looking at images on the internet, which later turned into watching porn.

It didn't take me long to get addicted to it.

Dealing with the emotional stress that came from being different and feeling abnormal made me run to the internet even more. Among other reasons it was extremely hard for me to talk to anyone about it and that only made my addiction worse.

Porn and online chat rooms turned into my drug, and in some seasons of life I'd be on the internet almost every night. I didn't like myself or what was going on inside my head, and I felt very lonely.

That turned out to be excellent soil for a destructive addiction. I did things I didn't want to do, and when no one was watching I turned into someone I didn't want to be.

Everyone saw me as a happy, good Christian boy but behind closed doors, I was someone else.

I felt like Dr.Jekyll and Mr.Hyde.

It ended up ruining my life. I wasted time that should have been spent with friends and family or doing homework (lol.) I was sleep deprived. I felt more depressed. I became more and more insecure.

I got really good at lying and such a pro at wearing different masks that I sometimes had a tough time figuring out who I really was.

Essentially I became someone I didn't want to be, and that should be reason enough to call in reinforcements, which leads me to the beginning of the answer to the equation.

The key was opening up to people.

Just like talking to my friends about my attractions to men was healing for me, so was opening up about my addiction to pornography. When I opened up about it, I was like Luke Skywalker going into the cave to face the Darth Vader inside of me.

I also started opening up to God about this stuff instead of running away from him. I learned to walk this journey with him and that he loves me with each step I take, whether it's forwards or backwards.

Jesus has radically transformed my life and is still walking with me today.

While my same-sex attractions haven't magically disappeared (as some church-folk expected them to) I choose not to pursue them and fight because I believe that God's ways are far higher than my own and that he has a plan for my life.

I learned that some monsters don't go away, they need to be faced and dealt with. Especially when they're your own.

Once I started being more transparent with my friends and family, my situation improved. I learned to be honest about mistakes, and allow others to help me figure out how to become the person I wanted to be.

If you're currently a lone wolf and you feel like Bruce Banner is no match for the Hulk, then here's my number one advice: Open up to someone; a friend, mentor, a family member etc.

The best way to win a battle is to get some allies. As I started talking to my friends about insecurities, emotional problems and porn I realised a lot of my allies needed me as much as I needed them.

You're not alone in this, so don't allow yourself to be.

PS: Sorry for all the pop culture references!

- Nils Arnell

Discussion questions

1. What was your first exposure to something ex-plicit?

2. Did you ever actively seek it out yourself? If so why?

3. What are the common triggers that lead you to watching porn?

4. What's your biggest takeaway from Nils' story?

THE WOLF

Chapter 5 - The Hunger of the Wolf

"Why did the wolf go for it?"

So you may be thinking...

"Wolves are smart, like really smart. They're one of the most cunning predators in the world. How on earth could it be so stupid?"

Simple: Because it was hungry.

'You're not yourself when you're hungry' as they say, so you can't judge the wolf too much.

It had an excuse.

After all our IQ levels can fluctuate based on factors like whether we are hungry, tired or even aroused.

"Oh, so that explains how someone as smart as me makes such... easy mistakes."

You betcha, Sherlock.

THE WOLF

The wolf went for the blade because it had a natural urge to eat (also known as an appetite...it helps us survive.)

The problem for our wolf is that this urge dominated its thoughts, taking priority above all other things. Even common sense like 'hey, don't lick that, it's a knife, you'll get cut.'

Many people wonder why they keep on making the same sexual mistakes again and again. Some even question why on earth they have these urges in the first place.

Before we jump in, here's a quick disclaimer for you guys:

This book is not anti-sex, instead it's very much the opposite.

Porn is sex are not the same thing.

This book is pro-sex, but it is, without a doubt, anti-porn.

There have been a lot of negative attitudes and stigmas in the church around the topic of sex (don't say that word!)

It's as if people fail to connect the dots that if they believe God created the world, then he also created sex (can we get an amen?)

Of course, there's a time and a place for everything. For example, the Bible claims that sex should be enjoyed in the context of marriage between a man and a woman.

By today's standards that seems laughable, but people often overlook the fact that the Bible isn't shy about addressing the matter of sex pretty explicitly.

When I started reading through the Bible, I was surprised at how many times sex was mentioned and how significant a role it plays in the stories.

From a secular perspective, the Old Testament reads more like a Game Of Thrones script than a typical Sunday morning church service.

Alongside this, you have the 'classic verses guaranteed to make your youth-worker uncomfortable' quoted predominately by snickering young lads in youth groups such as:

- *"your breasts are like two fawns, like twin fawns of a gazelle." (4:5)*
- *"the joints of thy thighs are like jewels" (7:1)*

"Wait... Surely these can't be in the Bible?"

Yup and that's just the tip of the iceberg.

'Song of Songs' is a cheeky wee book squeezed between Psalms and Proverbs written by a guy called Solomon, the King of Israel at the time and son of the famous King David.

Solomon's books are such an interesting read - especially for a 21st-century audience - because in the world's eyes he 'had it all:'

- King of one of the most powerful nations of his time.
- Wisest man in the world
- Rulers from all over the world came to him for advice.
- Richest man alive.

Plus his love life was interesting to say the least.

He had 700 wives and 300 concubines (basically prostitutes reserved for the king.)

Not exactly a great role model for relationships, (though some of you may disagree.)

'Mo lovers, mo problems.'

What's interesting is that a lot of his writings reflect the massive amount of problems this 'love life' caused him and we get to see the consequences of not sticking to the one-spouse system God established in Genesis.

In the end, this was one of the things that led to Solomon's ruin.

But God still used Solomon to do some incredible things. He was one of the many flawed people God raised up to be heroes.

One of the major things he did was write the books Proverbs, Song of Songs, and Ecclesiastes - three very crucial books in the Old Testament/Hebrew Bible which are still discussed and studied today.

Song of Songs is basically an erotic exchange of letters between two star-crossed lovers. While considered very romantic for its time, historical and cultural differences have made the book a little more... entertaining.

(If I described my wife Jaci's hair as being like a flock of goats it wouldn't go down so well.)

The meaning of the book is often debated, and throughout history, kids have been forbidden to read it until they got married.

The famous bible commentator Matthew Henry even claimed that:

"Jewish doctors advised their young people not to read it till they were 30 years old" lest they kindle *"the flames of lust."*

Wherever you stand on Song of Songs or the life of Solomon one thing is clear while reading the Bible:

God does not shy away from sex. Instead, He celebrates it.

The Bible is full of sex because it is a significant part of what makes us human.

Think about it: God could have created sex with no sensation involved - like brushing your teeth or eating a bowl of porridge.

He could have made it purely functional, e.g. to procreate/make babies, but he also made it pleasurable, both physically and emotionally.

However, on the other hand, the Bible does have a lot of laws, guidelines and principles to follow when it comes to sex.

As we go through this book we'lll take a look at both sides of this sexual equation to see how both can be true and how both are important.

"Hey I thought this was a book about porn, not a Bible lesson."

Don't worry; you haven't been click-baited.

I hear what you're saying, and if you couldn't care less about 'all that Christian stuff' that's fine. I recognise and understand that we don't all share the same worldview.

But just to be clear: in this book, I will be using the Bible as a framework to draw out principles that hopefully people from any faith (or lack of it) can use to overcome an unhealthy relationship with lust.

I'm neither a theologian or medical professional. This stuff isn't gospel truth; it is merely my experience/thoughts based on my own journey to freedom as a teen. Keep that in mind as we go forward.

"I mean I'll stay for a few more pages… Where do we start?"

The same place every great story does… 'in the beginning…'

Where Does 'The Hunger' Come From?

The Bible tells us that in the beginning there was a bloke named Adam.

He was the first person on the planet, placed into a beautiful paradise called the Garden of Eden, and may or may not have had a belly button.

(It's a real debate, Google it.)

Adam had what many of us daydream about: pure paradise.

But there was one problem:

He was lonely, and God noticed.

"It's not good for the man to be alone." - Genesis 2:18

What follows is a hilarious scene where God brings all the animals before Adam to see if any of them would make a good buddy.

"The man named the cattle, named the birds of the air, named the wild animals; but didn't find a suitable companion." - Genesis 2:20

I may have been tempted to settle for a tiger or a platypus because they're awesome, but Adam was still lonely (though he did get to name all the animals which is pretty cool.)

The hunt for Adam's bestie continued. God got his thinking cap on and seriously upped his game.

"God put the Man into a deep sleep. As he slept, he removed one of his ribs and replaced it with flesh. God then used the rib that he had taken from the Man to make Woman and presented her to the Man." - Genesis 2: 21-22

Talk about literally being made for each other. Sorry romcoms, but you can't beat that.

Adam's reaction? He set the trend that most young men now follow when they fall in love: **he burst into boyband style poetry.**

"Finally! Bone of my bone, flesh of my flesh!" - Genesis 2:23

OK... so it's not the catchiest jingle in the world, but you get the point. Adam finally found the one his soul loved, and he was lonely no more.

You see we are made for community. Even with the perfect paradise of Eden, Adam still wasn't satisfied with his life.

We have needs that cannot be met when we are on our own; some can only be met by others.

We can have all the material things in the world and still be left dissatisfied.

This need for community looks different for each of us.

For example, my wife Jaci, is an extrovert. She LOVES to be around people and feels energised when she is.

On the other hand, I'm an introvert. I don't mind being alone for extended periods of time, and in fact, I enjoy it. Being around people for too long can leave me feeling drained.

But, both of us NEED time with other people. Even an introvert like me starts to get crazy after long periods of time without community.

If you don't believe me and think you're some sort of lone wolf, all you have to do look at the fact that solitary confinement is used as a form of torture.

The results of it are devastating because it cuts off an essential human need.

Back in the day we humans lived in tight-knit communities in the forms of tribes, villages, and close families. Nowadays our society is quite disconnected, and as a result, our hunger for community can be left unsatisfied.

When any of our basic needs aren't met over a long period of time we tend to start to act irrationally.

What about you?

Has lust ever left you feeling dissatisfied?

Porn, masturbation, one-night stands, and casual dating relationships may 'meet' our need for connection... but only temporarily. In the end they left me feeling empty and shallow, often incredibly quickly afterwards.

They were a quick-fix to feel connected and loved, tricking me out of my loneliness only to plunge me into even greater isolation than before.

Social media can give us similar experience. All those likes and notifications create a feel-good effect or even the impression that people care about us.

But it's a blood-tipped blade in its own right, often causing us to feel more lonely, isolated, and disconnected in the end… especially when we overuse it.

In light of this, let's pause to allow a key truth settle into our hearts and minds.

There is nothing wrong with the need, the problem lies with how we try to meet it.

There is nothing wrong with the hunger, but rather what we feed on to fill ourselves up.

So why do we have this need?

I believe this hunger was given to us by God as something good.

It's healthy and important, just like how a wolf's God-given appetite urges it to hunt for food which in turn gives the wolf the energy it needs to survive.

The need for connection is a healthy appetite, not some sort of fatal flaw.

We as humans live better when we live together. Our appetite for community drives us to build cities, get married, make friends, join clubs, work on projects, solve problems and helps us THRIVE.

It drives us to live life together.

"Ok but what about sex?"

I'm glad you asked.

Sex is an incredible gift given to us by God with some great benefits, to say the least.

What a lot of people don't realise is that He designed it to be shared with a life partner. Someone who is committed to you until the end.

You see, porn and casual relationships don't care about you; they're not committed to you... (they ain't loyal!)

They are a selfish one-way transaction with their needs in mind, not yours.

They have no interest in you as a person or value for who you are.

They're a quick fix, like grabbing fast-food instead of taking the time to cook dinner.

(Which after eating we get hungry again super quick and feel worse even than we did before.)

Thus the cycle begins. But more on that later.

So who's hungry?

Well, a survey reveals that 79% of men and 76% of women between the ages of 18-30 watch porn at least once a month with a third of Americans actively seeking it out monthly.

(See https://www.barna.com/research/porn-in-the-digital-age-new-research-reveals-10-trends/)

This is a pretty conservative statistic compared to others floating around.

Clearly, there's a lot of hungry people in the world, and you ain't the only wolf in the forest.

"But Matt, you don't get it. Those people aren't like me; I have a real problem, I mean I'm hungry all the time!"

Fear not young wolf and believe me when I tell you that you're not alone.

You have a natural God-given appetite and sex drive (praise the Lord.)

You are a healthy, normal, hormone-stuffed young person (perhaps not so young.)

Relax, it's normal to have a sexual appetite. Stop freaking out about it.

However... it's important to acknowledge that just the like wolf, chances are we're not making the best choices with our diet.

"Our diet?"

Yes, our diet sucks.

Here's a well-known truth: donuts are delicious, but they're not good for us. *(why God, why?!)*

They're stuffed with sugary, fatty tastiness, and the more regularly we eat them, the more we crave them.

Our body gets hooked on the energy spikes and encourages us to eat donuts all the time.

(Sometimes our body is a little dramatic, like the wolf, it always has survival on its mind, even when starvation is unlikely.)

The good news is, when we cut out sugar and caffeine from our diet, we start to crave them less and less. But to get to that point, you have to journey through all the cravings and break the unhealthy habits.

However, the real problem with the donut diet is that we are filling up on rubbish (that's trash for any of you American readers) instead of what we actually need.

While we may feel full, the reality is that our needs are not met, and we go malnourished.

Pornography is like a donut sprinkled with cocaine.

We crave it because that's what we have been filling ourselves up on for years... yet we're baffled at how empty and dissatisfied we feel.

(Again, we're not the smartest sometimes.)

Chances are, a bad diet isn't a recent thing for us with most of us eating the wrong stuff for a very long time.

Sadly, some of us even from our childhood...

Have you ever seen the warnings on cigarette boxes discouraging pregnant women from smoking? Well, it makes sense, because it's not safe for the baby.

Toxic substances at such a crucial age of development can lead to deadly complications.

Or think about steak (yum.)

Is steak a bad thing?

"Uh yeah Matt, I'm a vegan."

awkward

Well, come with me anyway for the sake of the point.

Steak is a beautiful, delicious food, (for most of us,) but we would never dream of feeding steak to a newborn child.

Why? Because they're not ready to handle it.

A newborn child isn't developed enough to process a complex food like steak... heck they don't even have teeth.

Even if they somehow were able to swallow steak, it could do some serious damage.

That's why we feed our babies milk.

"Not if they're lactose intolerant"

^Point taken. #21stCentury^

I, like a lot of you, first stumbled upon porn at around 11 years old.

I wasn't seeking it out and without sounding too dramatic: **it found me.**

Here's the thing, many people see no harm in watching porn, and no one can stop you if that's what you wanna do.

But I think we all can agree that 11 years old is far too young. At that age, a lot of kids haven't even started their puberty phase. Someone that age can't possibly know how to process what they are looking at on the screen.

Most 11-year-olds still are afraid of catching 'cooties' or whatever the Americans call it.

Don't you remember being young and the thought of having a boy-friend or girlfriend was gross and weird?

To be honest, that's how most of us feel about porn at the start - gross and weird.

We clicked/swiped away quickly, freaked out by what we saw, and vowed never to do it again.

But, curiosity is a powerful thing. We went back for a second look, still grossed out but eager to learn what this is all about.

Then we got hooked, like wolves falling for the trap.

Sadly, the stats show that this is the story of most of us born in the smartphone age.

Generation XXX as they say: the first generation to grow up with access to any type of porn they want with just a few taps on a screen.

High-speed, hardcore content in our pockets. On demand. Whenever and wherever.

So what's the big deal?

I believe that early access to porn unlocks part of us prematurely before we are ready for it.

Like a baby eating steak, it's not that sexual attraction is a bad thing, it's just that it was bad timing.

I'm told that sexually abused kids can have their sexual nature awoken prematurely.

That something is kickstarted in a child before they are ready to handle it and that can lead to issues down the line.

I want to ask you a question.

Do you think it's possible that something similar can happen with early exposure to porn?

Seriously, what do you think?

This is heavy stuff I know, but I want to get the conversation going and ask some of these hard questions.

If this is your story, please know that this isn't the end of your journey or Game Over.

There is a way out, and it's more than possible to break the cycle.

Trust me; if a bunch of teens from Northern Ireland can do it you certainly can too.

I personally believe there is a lot more surrounding the issue of pornography and lust than what meets the eye.

(After all, the effect of mass-consumption of pornography can only be studied as our newer generations grow up.)

In my eyes, diet is only a small piece of the pie when it comes to all this stuff, and I'm excited to share some ideas with you.

You don't have to agree with me, but you can at least think it over. In the next chapter we're going to look at the **home of the wolf.**

How our culture and environment plays a key, but not an undoable role in all of this.

It's important we look at this before diving into the practical steps in **THE FIGHT.**

But first, here's another real-life story and some discussion questions for you to work through.

STORIES FROM THE WOLFPACK
- Jeff McIntosh: A Concerned Parent

There's another group out there that doesn't know how to handle the "new world" of porn.

The concerned parent.

My name is Jeff McIntosh. I have 2 children, currently aged 7 and 9.

We live in an odd point in history where fifth graders show Kindergartners porn on the bus, internet searches autofill pornographic titles of varying degrees and commercials are highly-sexualised

Content that would have been deemed unimaginable several decades ago are now blasted across every screen in America during the Super Bowl.

As result kids all over the nation and indeed the world are experiencing 'that first moment' that ends up defining their teenage years.

As a concerned father, I cannot yet formulate how we approach this issue with our kids.

The rules are the same as when we were kids, but the access is different.

Not only is it different, but unlimited.

After reading early copies of this book, I took a call to action and decided no-one would have access to pornography in my house.

I picked up the phone, called my cable and internet provider and told them I want to ensure no-one could access pornography from our home.

They said it was easy…

Great!

We logged on to the router, clicked into the right place, and they gave me the instructions:

"Type in any word you don't want to be accessed and if a website contains that word, it will be blocked."

Really!?

I had to come up with and type up every combination under the sun to protect my kids?

Surely there's got to be a better way.

Between home internet, YouTube, billboards and commercials, we are completely at a loss for how to limit the exposure our children will certainly face.

Our solution has been to keep the TV off and have computers in public places, but all we've done is created a bubble, that I'm sure will pop before we are ready.

We need help because we know the world of access is moving too fast for us to keep up with.

We also know sex sells to adults and there is no filter we can put on the world around us to keep our kids from exposure.

For now, we will keep praying with them, talking to them, praying for them, spending time with them and building trust with them.

Like every loving parent, we will take all the help we can get.

I'm grateful for all the young people in this book who have shared their story.

They are the key to solving this complex issue for the next generation because they have walked down paths we parents never did.

Let's be sure we listen to them.

Discussion Questions

1. Why do you think sexual issues can be such a taboo? (Something people don't want to discuss)

2. Have you ever felt like it was wrong to have a sexual appetite? If so, why?

3. Matthew was 11 years old when he first encountered porn. Did this shock you or can you relate to it?

4. What's your biggest takeaway from Jeff's story?

Chapter 6 - The Home of the Wolf

…Trouble in paradise.

Wolves look very different based on where they live.

For example, an arctic wolf has lighter fur than a wolf you'd find in the forest.

These differences are based on their environments. Where they live - their home - influences the wolves a great deal.

You see this with tame animals versus wild animals too. Even the average household dog is a force to be reckoned with out in the wild.

My trip to Nepal changed my view on 'mans best friend' forever. The wild dogs up the Himalayas were quite frankly… wild.

In fact, they seem like a different creature altogether compared to the cuties who snuggle next to you while you're watching Netflix.

It turns out, our environments play a significant role in our lives too.

THE WOLF

Here's a petty example:

I don't like rice very much. In fact, I try to avoid it when possible. However, because I am Northern Irish, I LOVE potatoes. (some stereotypes are true.)

On the other hand, I have friends who were born and raised in Asia that eat rice three times a day and have done so most of their life.

You know what they're not crazy about? Potatoes.

Here's a less petty example:

Jaci and I from two different countries, cultures, and families.

We both have an idea of the best way to do things - from small things like how to hang the washing to bigger things like how to raise kids (when they get here.)

The environments we grew up in still have an effect on us today, even though we haven't been living at home for 5+ years.

After our honeymoon, we'd constantly be having a laugh about how stubborn we were, even if it was something a trivial as the best way to wash the dishes.

Naturally we were both convinced our way was the best way.

I think what makes lust and porn such a complicated issue to talk about is the fact that everyone has an opinion.

Everyone thinks they have the answer and like Jaci and I, think their way is the best way.

It would be insane for me to write this book without discussing how our society and culture influence our relationship with lust.

But first, let's take a quick look at where we were designed to live… Again, let's go back to the beginning before looking at the present.

Paradise

That's what the Garden of Eden was.

Eden had some pretty awesome things going for it.

Here are a few ideas of what it may have looked like:

- Humans and animals lived in peace * high fives a lion *
- Healthy earth: no earthquakes, volcanoes, tsunamis etc.
- No sickness
- No guilt or shame
- No conflict between humankind (no war, divorce, etc)
- No clothes… (Certainly made choosing an outfit easy.)

Adam and Eve were given this paradise to enjoy with one simple instruction: *'Don't eat the forbidden fruit.'*

Easy peasy.

Right?

Spoiler alert

They broke the one rule and ate the fruit.

YOU HAD ONE JOB. Come on guys.

But in fairness, they didn't do it all alone…

The enemy came and hissed *'there's a better way... don't you guys want to be like God?'*

Unfortunately our lovebirds did and they fell for his trap.

Now, I know what you're thinking.

"Why did God make the rule in the first place?"

Again, this isn't a theology book, so I'll keep it brief (don't worry it's relevant to what we're going to get into.)

In short, if he hadn't they wouldn't have free will and without free will we'd just be fleshy robots, programmed to love a higher deity.

That's not real love. It's fake, and no one wants to be loved like this - especially not God.

They needed the ability to make a choice to be free, and unfortunately, they made the wrong one.

"Ahh, that makes sense now. But what happened next?"

A Poisoned Paradise

The moment our dynamic duo ate the forbidden fruit they were no longer innocent.

They realised what was right and wrong in the world and by their actions they opted out of God's planned paradise that he created just for them.

They were done with God running the show and wanted the keys to drive the car themselves…

The results were not pretty.

You see humans are great - like really great - we are even made in God's image.

Humanity is the crown of creation.
We're creative, beautiful, and unlike anything else God made.

We are a lot of great things... but we are not God.

Once Adam and Eve started running the show, things got out of hand fast.

Damage Report:

Responsibility #1: Water all the crops and feed all the animals.

Result #1: They couldn't. So the animals went wild, with no option but to hunt, kill and eat each other to survive.

Responsibility #2: Take care of the planet.

Result #2: Natural disasters and a sick earth.

Responsibility #3: Maintain peace on earth.

Result #3: They failed to do this, even within the family as sadly their eldest son killed the youngest.... Division, divorce, and war also became 'normal' over time.

Other side effects:

- They had to work the land to survive: enter stress, exhaustion and not having enough.

- They couldn't control or contain tiny bacteria or cells: enter sickness and disease.

- There was a separation between God and Man: We cut off the relationship with God when we ran away from home and tried to do things ourselves.

A lot of people blame God for the problems of the world, but aren't we really the ones to blame?

Poverty, hunger and war are all results of our failures as managers of the earth.

There's enough money, food and space in the world for everyone, yet the majority of the world lives without the basic essentials.

We poisoned the world, and now everyone who is born into it is poisoned too… corrupted by our own corruption.

We are naturally bent towards rebellion against each other and against God.

Evil is never something that is taught, rather it's now part of the human condition.

This is what you will hear Christians call 'sin.'

It's not just a 'naughty action' like sneaking a peep at something you shouldn't; it's much deeper than that.

It's the poison that seeped into our beings and our universe all because we went rogue.

"Bro, this got heavy quick! What can we do about it?"

Stick with me; I'm going somewhere with all this.

The Aftermath

Being born into the environment of this 'poisoned paradise' called earth affects us.

A lot of the reasons 'why we are the way we are' is simply a result of our home.

This means that we inherit beautiful traits like joy, love, laughter, creativity, communication and compassion but it also means that we inherit ugly things like anger, jealousy and lust.

Look at your own life, if you were lucky enough to know your parents you know that you have picked up good things and bad things from mum and dad.

The same with your friends and community. We pick up things from the people and places around us.

"How exactly does this help with my porn addiction?"

The point I'm trying to make is that a lot of our attitudes and habits around lust are largely a result of the world we live in.

In other words, it's not merely our fault alone.

Lust has always existed throughout the history of humanity... it's not some sort of new evil invention.

From the adultery of King David, mass-orgies in Rome, shrine prostitutes of pagan religions and Playboy magazines in the 70s all the way up to the websites we know today, lust has always been around.

Humans are sexual beings. We always have been and always will be and as discussed in the last chapter, we were created this way.

But just like Adam and Eve we often make the wrong choices.

This is pretty much what lust is - wrong choices - whether it's what we think about, what we watch, or what we do.

It's not a new thing. It existed for your parents, grandparents and all the way back to Adam.

But the way lust has presented itself over time, that indeed is interesting because it has changed quite dramatically in recent times - especially with the rise of the internet.

It's important to acknowledge that we are living in a very unique point in history when it comes to lust.

For the first time in human history, the common man/woman can summon anything their eyes desire to see with just a tap of a button.

This is a game changer.

Adam never faced this problem, nor did any other 'Adams' in history up until the last few years.

Even a man like King Solomon who had the world at his fingertips didn't have access to this.

There are few other unique things we face today in the 21st Century.

Let's take a look at some.

1. We are bombarded with sexual images daily

From YouTube ads, to social media posts to good old-fashioned billboard/TV adverts - we are presented with a wide variety of sexual images on a daily basis.

The average person is exposed to hundreds of ads every day, many of which contain sexual elements because as we all know; sex sells.

Advertisers know they can tap into the needs we talked about earlier and try to sell a solution for that, a solution that doesn't work and leaves us hungry.

Most of us have become so used to it that we hardly even notice anymore.

In other words: hyper-sexual has become 'our normal.'

It's no longer odd to see sex being used to sell buildings, burgers and everything in-between.

I wasn't aware of what we are exposed to on a daily basis until I started to work towards my own freedom.

As I was trying to cut out 'lusty stuff' from my life (change my diet) it was easy to feel like there was nowhere to hide.

Back to donuts: imagine if a donut addict was constantly bombarded with ads for donuts on phones, TVs, trains, airports, magazines and streets.

It would makes it kinda hard for them to stay away from donuts right?

Most of us are visually minded, and advertisers use this to their advantage because we do a pretty good job of remembering images - especially sexual images.

(Test: do you remember the first pornographic material you were exposed to?)

A lot of emphasis has been put on how this visual nature is more dominant in men, but by no means is it exclusive to males. It's a very powerful thing for both sexes.

I used to see this trait as a curse, but now I have come to celebrate it.

While I haven't found any solid theory of why we have this visual nature, there is one suggestion.

Perhaps the ability to recall memories/images helped promote loyalty to our families when we would go out to hunt, fight in wars, and travel for extended periods of time across vast distances.

It would discourage people from just abandoning their family back home and setting up elsewhere.

I guess before iPhones and photographs there was no real way to carry a visual memory of your partner/family except in your mind.

Keeping those images of who you have back home could end up being a real motivation and source of inspiration.

It's why soldiers carry lockets of their lovers and truckers stick a photo on the dashboard.

Unfortunately, this is being used against us today, our visual nature is being reverse engineered to hurt us rather than help us.

You see for the majority of history the only real sexual images people would have been exposed to were in their bedroom with their spouse.

Plus, you were only exposed to these images once you hit the age of marriage and not often before.

But today, most of us are exposed to such images before we even get out of bed in the morning and kids are exposed way before they mature.

Today, our social media feeds are littered with types of pictures we would have previously only seen in the context of our marital bed.

Isn't that crazy?

Now a husband has to fend off the images of a thousand women to keep his thoughts on his wife.

Now a teen lying in bed at night has videos replaying in their head when all they want to do is sleep.

Now the young girl who watches porn believes that what she sees is normal, that this is how she must act, look and behave to be seen as beautiful in this world.

These are the images that captivate our eyes and our memories.

This is the environment that we have grown up in.

2. Attitudes towards loyalty have changed

For most of human history, you couldn't pursue a romantic relationship with someone unless you were married (or else you'd risk facing insanely serious consequences.)

This meant no dating, no casual chit-chat and no getting to know someone intimately other than your spouse - it was intense.

In fact, to have a sexual relationship outside of marriage ran the risk of punishment to the point of death.

These days, casual dating, hooking up and getting divorced are all highly acceptable practices that are even encouraged in some modern societies.

Now, pretty much half of all marriages end in divorce because it's viewed as something we can opt-in or out of when things get tough.

In the big picture of human history, this is pretty unique - not saying it has never happened before - but it certainly has changed dramatically in the past 100 years.

I am no marriage expert, nor am I saying that there aren't situations where divorce/separation should occur, but I think it's fair to say that our societal views on loyalty have changed drastically.

This lack of loyalty opens up more possibility and makes a spouse watching porn or flirting with a co-worker 'not a big deal.'

Back in the day, if you wanted to have sex your options were: sleep with your spouse, sleep with a prostitute or have a super risky affair.

Ancient Adam was limited to sleeping with one person or else paying some serious consequences (a fatal STD and/or a societal punishment,) whereas today, Adam is admired if he sleeps with multiple people.

Having sex with someone used to come with the commitment of taking care of and living with that person for the rest of your life.

Nowadays you may not even be expected to pay for dinner.

Sex is one of the greatest things that two people can share.

In addition to the physical connection, there's an extremely powerful emotional bond created when involved in a sexual relationship.

This is why a divorce, break-up or even a one-night stand can be such an emotionally devastating event.

What about you?

Have you been heartbroken due as the result of a break-up?

A lot of us are hurting due to a lack of loyalty, whether it was the break-down of one of our own relationships or the relationships of our parents.

Now the past was far from perfect - fear played a huge role and people faced horrific consequences.

While I'm not saying we should bring them back, I am pointing out that the current day holds possibilities that generally (and of course there are historical exceptions) we didn't even have access to.

All of us at any given time can access any type of sexual encounter we desire, almost instantly.

Times have certainly changed - even in just 30 years.

No longer do we have to sneak around our older brother's bedroom to rip out pages or venture into a shady store to get a hold of the 2D images found in magazines.

THE WOLF

Waiting hours for the download of a large video file is a thing of the past due to high-speed internet and streamable content.

For many, a lifelong commitment to someone before engaging in a physical relationship seems more like a quaint fairytale rather than an option to consider.

Talk about no strings attached. All it takes is a few taps and a swipe of a screen.

Our culture celebrates this freedom, but in my eyes, it has created more bondage than liberation.

I say this because I know me.

I know my flaws and I know that I can't trust myself with this type of power or responsibility.

I'm the guy who doesn't buy donuts for the house because if they're in the cupboard, I will most certainly eat them (all of them.)

There's no judgement here.

I'll be the first person to acknowledge that our environment is toxic and it seems like everywhere we go - there's no escape.

But it's not all doom and gloom.

There are plenty of positive things that have been allowed to flourish as a result of this.

In today's society, there is much more room for openness and expression.
This means that people who have sexual problems are more likely to speak out and get the help they need.

Plus sex being less of a taboo subject is great news for accountability (something we will talk a lot about later in THE FIGHT section.)

Secrecy is the breeding ground for bondage, guilt and shame. Being able to open up and talk about these things leads to freedom.

News Flash: You are more than your environment

Many great men and women throughout history have fought hard to overcome lust and addictions.

If they can do it - we can too.

Yes, the battle looks different than ever before.
Yes there are some new challenges that we face.

But victory is still there for those who have the courage to fight.

For those not willing to simply be a product of their environment.
For those who long to rise above what society tries to tell them to be.

Freedom and purity are there for the taking, but you have to fight for it.

Ladies and gentlmen, it's time for the main event.

Welcome to THE FIGHT.

STORIES FROM THE WOLFPACK
- Jacqueline Thompson: Nurse

Who are you?

Hi, my names Jaci, I'm a nurse originally from Germany and I'm Matt's wife!

What's your experience with porn/lust?

My only experience with porn was when I was around 12 years old.

My bestie and I thought we'd just look it up online as we heard about it but didn't understand what it was.

We just clicked on the first page that came up and were surprised that a message popped up asking if we were 18 years or older, we giggled to ourselves and clicked yes.

The page opened and there where images of naked woman. We didn't really get what was going on so we closed the page and moved on.

Going through my teenage years, I ignorantly assumed it was just men that struggled with lust and porn addictions.

Looking back on it now, I'm sure some of my female friends were hurt by things I must have said in my ignorance.

It was such an eye opener for me to hear some of my close female friends share their struggle in recent years and to learn how to encourage them and love them well in their walk towards freedom.

When Matt and I first met we were both working for a ministry in NYC and hosted a lot of short-term mission teams (mostly teenagers.)

He would share his story when asked and it was so beautiful to see so many young people finally having someone slightly older who said 'me too I've been there but there is a way out.'

What impact do you think porn is having on our culture?

I don't even know if we can comprehend yet, how this generation will be impacted in the long term - but it is definitely being educated by porn and that sadly will filter into how they treat their partners.

Some of my married friends are struggling in this area, and it's really such a strain in their relationship with their partner.

It feels like someone else is third-wheeling and has access into some of their most intimate areas.

I can't imagine the hurt and pain that must cause.

What would you say to the spouses reading this book?

If you are a bit like me (someone that had very little idea how this struggle can affect a person you love) choose to love well, show mercy and learn to be your partners biggest fan in the fight.

I can testify what a blessing it is and how much peace it brings into our marriage knowing my husband is not bound by those struggles anymore.

I am not perfect, and there are areas in my life, I need to grow and fight.

But in the area of lust my husband has grown so much, and he is choosing to share so openly and to ensure you know there is hope.

My job is to be his biggest fan.

So if you are the spouse cheering on - I encourage you to choose to fight alongside your partner, to celebrate the small wins, to speak life, to support to show grace and to pray for them.

The journey is so worth it.

If you are young, single and struggling with a porn addiction, I would encourage you to keep on fighting.

Who knows, maybe one day your future-spouse will thank you for it.

- Jaci

Discussion questions

1. In what ways is it more difficult to fight lust in your generation compared to your grandparent's generation?

2. In what ways is it easier?

3. How can you try and protect your visual diet in a culture dominated and obsessed with sex?

4. What's your biggest takeaway from Jaci's story?

THE FIGHT

Chapter 7 - The Wolf's Code

Welcome to THE FIGHT.

The FIGHT is the part of the book where we start to lay out some steps you can take to fight against this thing.

We'll break it up into 3 chapters:
- The Wolf's Code (fighting the battle in mind)
- Defend The Den (fighting the battle in the physical)
- Assemble a Wolfpack (fighting the battle alongside others)

In his essay Nature, Ralph Waldo Emerson said that *"an action is the perfection and publication of thought."*

This is relevant for us because lust always starts in the mind.

The wolf's code is a collection of principles we can live by to stop lust in its tracks before it manifests itself physically.

Learning how to deal with it there really helps set us up for success in our road to freedom.

The following chapter contains frameworks and ways of thinking that really helped me in my own FIGHT for purity.

Take from them what you will.

1. Purity is a lifestyle, not a pill

When it comes to exercise, we all want to get a shredded 6 pack in 20 days or pop a magic pill and wake up like Peter Parker post-spider bite.

The reality is however that it takes years of dedication diet and training and most of us can't be bothered with this, so we give up and settle for our one-pack (guilty.)

The people who have the most success with exercise aren't those who jump into some insane program and work out for 20 days straight (only to relapse back to their own ways.)

It's the folks who are consistent and make it their lifestyle to live healthy that achieve their goals.

Well, it's the same with our lust.

How many times have we made a "this is the last time" commitment only to last 3 days (and that's being pretty optimistic.)

If we are to make purity a reality for our lives, we need to accept that it is a lifestyle, not a quick fix.

Victory requires a long-game strategy and for us to start making small consistent changes now that will follow us the rest of our lives.

Don't wait for the overnight transformation, start fighting today.

It doesn't matter how many times you've failed or if you never even fought before, because as long as we are fighting, we are winning.

Freedom will come at some point, but it's not the victory in itself.

The victory is actually continuing to fight, no matter how many times you fall.

Check us this excerpt from a speech Theodore Roosevelt gave often labelled 'The Man In the Arena.'

He puts it so much better than I ever could.

"It is not the critic who counts; not the man who points out how the strong man stumbles, or where the doer of deeds could have done them better. The credit belongs to the man who is actually in the arena, whose face is marred by dust and sweat and blood; who strives valiantly; who errs, who comes short again and again, because there is no effort without error and shortcoming; but who does actually strive to do the deeds; who knows great enthusiasms, the great devotions; who spends himself in a worthy cause; who at the best knows in the end the triumph of high achievement, and who at the worst, if he fails, at least fails while daring greatly, so that his place shall never be with those cold and timid souls who neither know victory nor defeat."

It's time to get into the arena because it's the only place victory can be found.

2. Don't listen to the marriage myth

There's a gimmick floating around in Church circles that has got to be the biggest scam in regards to lust.

"Just wait until you get married, then all this will go away."

Lol.

If we're having 'sex' outside of marriage now ('sex' being used a very broad term here) why on earth do we think we're not going to have 'sex' outside of marriage later on?

It's almost as ridiculous as this one:

"If you masturbate it gets rid of all those urges and lets you experience purity..."

Hah!

Yeah, for like 3 minutes.

Chances are even the best sex life in the world couldn't keep up with most masturbation habits.

"Nah dude, when I get married we're going to have so much sex, you don't need to worry about that."

Oh yeah? So what happens when your partner says no, or can't have sex because of sickness, depression or tiredness?

The harsh reality is we would run the risk of jumping straight back into our old habits and put our marriage on the rocks in the process because we haven't learned to tame the hunger.

Because we didn't deal with our lust while we were single.

This is no game. The enemy is out to destroy marriages and tear families apart over this issue, and unfortunately, we are no exception.

Don't bank on the lie that once you start having regular sex all your lust problems will go away.

They won't, and many married men and women have discovered that the hard way.

Deal with it now, don't put it off, your future family will thank you for it.

This is why purity matters. This is why we fight.

3. Feed the right wolf

An old Native American legend claims that 2 wolves live inside of each of us.

A good wolf and an evil wolf.

The thought is that by our actions we decide which wolf gets fed and grows stronger.

For example, if we are continually treating other people with hate the evil wolf will grow and become the strongest, filling our lives with even more hate.

Or by constantly being generous our 'good wolf' is fed which in turn helps us to become even more generous.

This is a pretty neat concept, and it works well in relation to lust.

In a porn context the two wolves we face are 'lust' and 'purity.'

The more we feed the 'lust wolf' by watching porn/fantasizing/ acting out, the more powerful it becomes in our life.

The problem most of us face when we come to try and quit is that our 'purity wolf' is like a puppy in comparison to the lust monster we've been feeding for years.

Change your diet and watch that wolf begin to starve. Start cutting out anything in your life that causes you to lust bit by bit and see how much stronger purity becomes in your life.

Be aware of where your eyes fall in your everyday life - a diet can take a while to kick in- but making small steps day by day can make a massive impact on the future.

Whatever you starve shirnks. Whatever you feed grows.

4. Everything is permissible but not beneficial

This is a good one because most of us live our lives asking this question:

"How far can I go without going too far?"

But this is what the perspective of a loser looks like, not the mindset of a fighter or a victor.

Let's be sneaky and answer a question with another question:

"Can a man scoop flames onto his lap and not get burnt?" (Proverbs 6:27)

Honestly stop to think about it.

Can I handle lust?
Do I have a good track record with it?
Am I good at controlling myself when it comes to these types of stuff?

I think that right across the board, lust is a weak spot for most of society.

We all know people affected by it and people who have been hurt as a result of it being mismanaged: from presidents to parents.

Bill Perkins puts it this way:

"If you think you can't fall into sexual sin, then you're godlier than David, stronger than Samson, and wiser than Solomon."

It's so true, but where do we draw the line?'

There's a lot of seemingly 'grey area' in the Bible when it comes to stuff like dating, holding hands, kissing, masturbating, oral sex etc.

Nowhere in the Bible does it say "thou shalt not pleasure thyself."

However, the apostle Paul gives us a useful little nugget of wisdom to keep us on track when it comes to these issues.

"I have the right to do anything," you say - but not everything is beneficial. "I have the right to do anything" - but not everything is constructive." - 1 Corinthians 10:23

Paraphrase: Everything is permissible, but not everything is beneficial.

I imagine that every youth group on the planet would love to ask:

- *"Hey Paul, can I watch this explicit movie in the cinema?"*
- *"Hey Paul can I stay over at my boyfriends house?"*
- *"Hey Paul is it cool if me and my girlfriend make out for hours?"*

None of these have explicit 'Bible answers,' but I think Paul would turn round and answer them with:

"Well, everything is permissible, but not everything is beneficial."

Just because something isn't technically wrong, or 'not a sin' doesn't mean we should go ahead and do it.

Stop playing the sin counting game and instead ask yourself:

- *"Does this benefit my fight for purity?"*
- *"Ok, this isn't a sin… but could it lead me to sin?"*
- *"Does this decision push me forward, or pull me back?"*

This is how you think like a fighter. This is the game changer.

The question shouldn't be *"how close can I get to lust without it consuming me?"* It should be *"how far can I run towards purity to keep me on track?"*

5. Break the legs of the horses

Ok so this is a pretty brutal metaphor, but maybe it will work for some of you.

In Joshua chapter 11 there's a story where God tells the Israelites to break the legs of the enemies horses so they can't chase after them.

I've found it to be a pretty good principle to apply to our fight for purity.

You see, lust has many different 'horses,' but if we break the legs of those horses, it cripples them and stops them from running wild.

Here are some examples.

Again, take from them what you will...

Instagram

If you get sucked into a porn via a rabbit hole click trail from the Instagram explore page, then you need to cripple that horse in your life and close your account/delete the app.

"But I love my gram dude! I get like 100 likes every photo."

Ok great, but is it worth your purity?

Sexting

If you always sext the same person when you're feeling down, then it's time to block that contact and say "BYE FELICIA."

"But what if I genuinely need to contact that person about something?"

How many genuine reasons have you had in the last month to contact them that someone else couldn't have done?

Locks on the bedroom door

If you always lock the door before you watch porn, go ahead and rip that lock off your door.

"But I need my personal space! I'm an introvert like you Matt!"

Yeah, and chances are you a lust problem like I did. How's those locks working out for you?

I'm being overly dramatic intentionally here, but you have to admit there are elements of truth in these examples (and how whack the excuses we make up are.)

You see 'our horses' represent things that trigger us, and they can take many shapes and forms.

Once we start removing the triggers from our lives, it makes the FIGHT much easier and levels the playing field a little.

It's hard to outrun a horse, but it's easy to outrun a horse that can't run.

6. Get off the train before the doors close

In NYC I always used to take the A train on the subway. It's an express train, so it skips over a lot of smaller stops to make it faster.

When you're in downtown Manhattan, it stops around every 10 blocks… 34th St, 42nd, but once it got to 59th it would run express to 125th St.

If you didn't get off in time then you were stuck riding the train all the way up to 125th. Even if you wanted to get off in Central Park on 89th st, you couldn't because the doors were closed and you had no choice but to ride it.

If I were to say: *'the point of no return'* would that resonate with you?

That's how I describe the point where deep down you have committed to watching porn, masturbating or whatever else.

The point where there is no turning back, the point where the train doors close.

You see there are plenty of opportunities for us to get off that train before we reach that point - we just don't take them - because if we're honest, sometimes we don't actually want to.

The warning signs are always there:

- *We get click baited onto progressively more explicit sites…*
- *We take off their shirt…*
- *We stand up to lock the door…*

Then afterwards we are gobsmacked saying *"I mean I just don't know what happened!"*
- *"I was just shopping online."*
- *"We were just watching a movie."*
- *"I was just tidying my room."*

"How did I end up:"
- *"Watching porn?*
- *"Having sex with someone when deep down I didn't want to?"*
- *"Masturbating?"*

The reality is, we ignored the alarm bells and didn't get off the train when we had the chance.

Here's another example.

Run Joseph Run

In the Bible, there was a good-looking lad named Joseph.

Joseph's boss had a beautiful wife who had the hots for Jo and desperately wanted to sleep with him.

After making a few sly, failed attempts to get Joseph in bed she came up with a plan.

Basically, she waited for her husband to go on a business trip, gave all the other staff a day off and made sure it would just be her and Joseph alone in the house…

Que the Marvin Gaye music and the candles.
Well, Joseph showed up, realised what was going on and when

she made a move towards him you know what he did?

HE RAN FOR HIS LIFE.

You see Potiphar's wife would have been an attractive woman and Joseph a young man with a sex drive like the rest of us. He knew he if he stayed any longer he'd be in bed with her faster than you could say "run Joseph run."

He knew his weaknesses, he knew if he stayed any longer he'd give in, so he burst out the door and removed himself from the situation...

He got off the train before it was too late.

We can do the same by:
- *Closing our laptop.*
- *Deciding to leave.*
- *Simply walking out the door and going downstairs/out of the house.*

I know this sounds like really basic advice, but you'd be surprised how removing yourself from the situation can make all the difference.

Give it a go and remember:

The early you get off the train, the easier it is.

7. Self-control is not a gift

For many years I would constantly pray for self-control.

I prayed that God would take away my addiction and 'give me a will-power of steel.'
These are all good things and great prayers but guess what?

Self-control is not **'a gift of the spirit.'**

Nowhere in the Bible does it say that God will just magically give us self-control.

However, self-control is described as **'a FRUIT of the spirit.'**

Fruit doesn't just magically appear, it takes time to grow and ripen.

I think it's the same with the fruit of the spirit.

There's no *self-control magic drug* you can pop or prayer you can say, but rather it's a characteristic and strength that can be built up over time.

We build it up by walking in discipline and obedience to God in the small things as well as the big ones every day.

Stop expecting to wake up and your addiction to be gone and start walking on a journey to do something about it.

That may sound like I'm being harsh and cruel. I assure you I'm not.

I know how difficult of a situation you are in.

But I also know how I played the victim for so long instead of proactively doing something about it.

8. Porn ruins your sex life

Over the past few years, there has been a massive movement of young men OUTSIDE of the church, who are not even remotely religious starting to rebel against porn…

Why?

BECAUSE THEIR SEX LIVES SUCKED.

Premature ejaculation, erectile dysfunction and the inability to be with a real-life person physically are all reported side-effects of excessive porn consumption.

(See any of Gary Wilson's incredible research or TED Talk on this topic.)

Guys who had grown up with porn started to discover a couple of shocking things when they began having sex:

- They were lasting seconds in bed because they had trained themselves to climax quickly.

- They couldn't achieve/sustain an erection because they had conditioned themselves to respond to images on a screen and to their own hand.

- They were terrible lovers because they were selfish, impatient and frustrated when they didn't get the same response from their partners that they had seen in videos.

All of this leads to performance anxiety and low self-confidence.

I'll point out again that a lot of men and women now part of the anti-porn movement are liberal, anti-Christian and college-aged, a demographic you may automatically assume wouldn't have an issue with porn or the consumption of it.

They became fighters not because they wanted to be 'good Christians' but because they literally just wanted to have better sex lives.

The NoFap Reddit movement has millions of people from all over the planet from every walk of life imaginable banding together in an attempt to overcome their addictions to pornography and masturbation.

This isn't just a problem for the church, it's a problem for all of us.

In fact, it's even an issue for porn stars.

Check out this excerpt from The Butterfly Effect.

The interview takes place between Jon Ronson (the journalist) and Mike (a porn director.)

Both had been on the set of a porn shoot the day before, and Jon noticed something that shocked him.

Jon: *Some of the men who were finding it hard to sustain erections were watching porn to try and get erections… So there was [a naked female porn star] in the middle of the room and all the men were looking at their phones… It made me wonder if this was like a big societal change?*

Mike: *I think it is. That's all the evidence you need. There's a live woman in front of you, you can't get an erection, hold on a second while I [look at porn] you know? That's a statement.*

(Names of actors and names of websites removed by me.)

9. Porn's not real

Something we often fail to realise is that porn stars are actually actors.

That they perform a role for the camera in the same way a Hollywood movie star plays a character and takes on a persona that isn't really them.

What we see on the screen isn't real, from the plastic surgery to the exaggerated responses.

A lot of mainstream porn isn't simply a camera recording people having sex (though user-generated content and Amateur porn is on the rise.)

It's a full-scale production that is usually is made by a professional crew that utilise editing and camera angle tricks combined with a performance from the actors to put on a show.

To create something that is false.

This can lead to serious issues when people get down to have real-sex:

- Men + women think their bodies are inadequate compared to the unrealistic standard they see on screen.

- Many feel like they can't please their partners properly.

- People can attempt to recreate what they see on-screen which can range from impossible all the way to abusive.

Our generation has turned to porn to teach us about sex, and frankly, that's about as smart as going to a penguin to learn how to fly.

It's not real, and it can ruin real-life sex - one of the greatest gifts God has given humanity.

Again, please remember, being anti-porn does not mean being anti-sex.

It's actually probably the most pro-sex thing you can do and is something that both the church and secular world are paying attention to.

10. Hollywood killed love

This may seem like a little off topic, but it's an important thing to note.

Not only has the media in general sold us a lie about sex, but also a lie about love (yes the two are very different.)

Real life relationships take a lot of work and commitment. Things aren't a fairytale all the time.

Romance does not equal love.

The time will come in your relationship where one of you (or both) will have projectile diarrhea and vomiting.

Try putting that on Instagram #bae #squadgoals

Hard seasons will come, and if your relationship is built on romance then it's like the man who built his house on the sand... One big storm later and say goodbye to your home.

If marriage is indeed part of the plan for your life, then be aware that to achieve all the beauty and power of marriage will also require work and sacrifice.

In some areas, divorce rates are as high as 60%... that's not an easy number to ignore.

In our culture, if we don't like something we return it. If something breaks we buy a new one. If our marriages are no longer like a fairytale? Our society tells us to just get a new one.

This is the culture we are a part of, keep this in mind as you move forward.

Divorce and porn-consumption affects the majority of the population.

The MAJORITY.

Think about that for a second.

More people are struggling with these issues than people who don't.

That's why we should be careful taking any advice from our culture because it's clearly not working out for us as a society.

In his podcast about debt, Dave Ramsey always says *"if you want to live like no one else, then you have to live like no one else."*

That can be applied to more than just our finances.

Rising above these statistics requires us to live differently than the majority of the world lives.

It requires us to go against the popular way and to swim against the current.

Hollywood tries to sell us a whole bunch of ideas, but take a look at Hollywood and see the fruit of them.

Does it look like it's working?

Do the recent and ongoing scandals of sexual abuse make you wish you had their lives?

When we see how unhappy these people are… do we truly feel jealous?

Keep this in mind when the world pushes back against you.

Few of us truly want to become like the people we idolise when we break it down this way.

11. Keep the toothpaste in the tube

Have you ever splurged out way too much toothpaste and tried to put it back in the tube?

It's pretty much impossible.

Here's a scenario for you, maybe it will be a familiar one…

Once upon a time, there was a lovely young couple (let's say 13 years old) called Jimmy and Sarah. They met at school, thought each other were cute, and after a few weeks Sarah asked Jimmy out on a date over Snapchat.

They were obviously madly in love instantly.

It was their 4th date, they were going to the movies, and Jimmy had decided it was time.

Today was the day he would HOLD SARAH'S HAND.

Halfway through the movie he slipped out to empty his nervous bladder, psych himself up in the mirror and wash his hands to make sure they were hand-holding ready.

"You got this dude," he said to his reflection before storming back inside.

THE FIGHT

After sitting back down in his seat, he anxiously began to execute his plan. Strategically placing the popcorn box in between them, he waited for the emotional peak of the movie. The music blared, the characters were reconciling, the lady behind them started to cry, and Sarah put her hand into the popcorn box (even though there wasn't much popcorn left.)

Seamlessly Jimmy went in for the popcorn, brushed his hand against hers and slowly took her by the hand. Sarah blushed, Jimmy's heart was about to explode and lovely lovey-dovey chemicals flooded through their bodies at a million miles an hour. They looked at each other shyly and sweetly, smiles beaming from their face…

2 weeks later they held hands everywhere they went and didn't give two thoughts about it.

THE END.

From that moment on, Jimmy and Sarah picked up right where they left off. What was once a huge deal to them was no longer exciting or stimulating.

This progression is normal and natural.

However, when Jimmy and Sarah break up, they will typically hold hands with their new partners much faster because it's not the same ordeal it was before.

Sure it's exciting and novel because it's a new person, but it's just not the same.

The toothpaste was out of the tube and it couldn't be put back in.

Now, what happens if we take the same scenario only make Jimmy and Sarah 18 years old, and change the hand holding to sex. Sarah and Jimmy are now much quicker to jump in bed with new partners which can lead to problematic things like:

- Moving too quickly in new relationships and putting pressure on new partners

- A casual 'one night stand lifestyle'

- Numbness to stimulation creating the need to go further and further to get the same buzz.

While it's possible for things to get seriously out of hand between people in the real world, the digital world has even fewer limitations leaving an unlimited potential to skip through each stage at a faster rate.

Few people start with hardcore porn - they naturally build up to it - they let the toothpaste out a little at a time, picking up where the left off each time.

Our brain gets bored very quickly and requires new novel stimulation to get the same kick as the last time. This can lead to some insane online habits that quickly delve into the realm of being criminal and punishable by law.

It's a progression that if left unchecked can take you places you never imagined you could go.

Stop the progression.

Don't squeeze any more toothpaste out of the tube, because you will find it very difficult to put it back in.

It takes time, and it takes healing.

It's possible, but it may take a while.

That's why it's important we don't let any more out so we can allow the healing process to take place.

Memories fade. Habits change.

It just takes time.

12. It's the second glance that binds you

At some points in my journey to freedom, I was incredibly critical of myself.

I didn't treat myself with love, kindness or gentleness. I was angry and ashamed of this part of my life and treated it with rage and contempt.

This didn't help.

I was too focused on trying to reach the destination rather than embracing the journey and committing to the process.

Something I failed to realise was that there is a difference between appreciating beauty and lusting.

I was so obsessed with guarding my eyes and controlling my 'diet' that I felt angry and disappointed in myself if I even noticed a woman I found attractive.

It was only a few years after my breaking my addiction that I began to experience healing in this area of my life.

There are a lot of beautiful things in this world. From nature to art to people.

Newborn children are beautiful. A couple on their wedding day is beautiful.

An attractive young man or woman is beautiful.

This is a reality. It is true.

But because I had been burnt by lust, I was afraid of beauty.

When on the bus, bicycle or subway you will always come across beautiful people.

That's part of life, and there is nothing wrong with that.

You will see someone walk into your shop, work or church and think: *"wow they are really beautiful."*

There's nothing wrong with it. Accept the fact, acknowledge it and move on.

When we agressively beat beauty down in our minds and make a massive deal out of it, we give it more power and attention than it needs or deserves.

After all, when God sat back and looked at creation in Genesis, he acknowledged that it was good. We should do the same.

I often define lust in my own life as 'the second glance.'

It's when we intentionally go for a 2nd or 3rd or 4th glance and begin to obsess over beauty that isn't ours to have.

This is true both online and offline, with someone right in front of us or someone in our minds/on screen.

Casting Crowns phrases this perfectly in their song Slow Fade.

"It's the second glance that ties your hands, as darkness pulls the string."

The first glance is fine. In fact, it's normal. You can't just not look at or notice people. Wearing blinders or not making eye contact with everyone in life isn't a realistic option.

But it's the second glance we need to look out for.

That's where beauty can be twisted into lust.

There's nothing wrong with thinking that someone is attractive. What matters is what happens after that point.

13. There are bigger fish to fry

Look here's the deal - lust issues have the potential to affect every area of our lives - but we need to keep one thing in mind.

The hunters would want nothing more than for this to define you. For this to become everything that you are.

One of the greatest tactics the hunters use in our day and age is to try to get us to associate a desire or behaviour we have with our identity.

I'm obviously a huge advocate for you overcoming your addiction... but be careful not to give it too much power in your life.

If giving up porn becomes the ultimate thing in your life, your idol or identity, then the chances are you probably won't beat it.

I know that seems bizarre, but when you make this your everything you can start to view it as an arm or a leg (part of who you are) instead of a tumour (an external part of yourself.)

No one mourns over the loss of a tumour, but the loss of a limb is devastating.

Please let these words resonate with you:

This is not who you are. This is not your identity. This does not define you.

Don't make this your ultimate thing.

That's what the hunters want. They want you to spend all your attention on them and their traps.

Don't give them that.

When asked about what the most important commandment is Jesus gave a simple and clear answer:

"The most important commandment is this: 'Listen, O Israel! The Lord our God is the one and only Lord. And you must love the Lord your God with all your heart, all your soul, all your mind, and all your strength.' The second is equally important: 'Love your neighbor as yourself.' No other commandment is greater than these." - Mark 12:29-31

Put simply: Love God with your everything and love people the way you want to be loved.

This is and always should be your highest priority, because that's what the head of the pack says is most important.

Keep your head up.

Keep walking forward.

You will beat this thing, but until then you are still you, you are still an awesome man/woman of God, and you are still created in his image.

"Look these are cool and all, but surely there's more than just lofty principles to help me, what about practical, real-life, real-world stuff we can do?"

You're right. Talk is cheap and action matters.

But don't let these just wash over you. I always found it was the principles that kept everything else in place.

In the next chapter we'll talk about physical steps we can take to defend the den.

Hope to see you there.

STORIES FROM THE WOLFPACK
- Rebecca Hodge: Counsellor

"The biggest sex educator of young men today is pornography, which is increasingly violent and dehumanizing, and it changes the way men view women." - Dr Gail Dines Professor of Sociology and Women's Studies.

Who are you?

My name is Rebecca Hodge, I'm a Counsellor, advocate against human trafficking and a proud mum of two!

What effect do you think pornography is having on our society?

The effect of pornography on our society is a phenomenon I have considered and researched for a number of years.

In my professional life, I've encountered the sad and destructive effect of porn in the lives of clients.

I see how it destroys, deceives and damages relationships, individuals, families and communities…often crossing the religious and secular divide.

I believe there's an undeniable link between pornography and sex trafficking, and wonder how, in a society where so many are now standing against this sexual slavery, many are comfortable with porn which is a gateway to a dark and twisted view on human value.

Why do you think so many of us turn to porn?

Porn is an internet epidemic, and where there is demand, there will always be supply.

Considering that in 2015 there were reportedly over two billion internet searches for porn, it is evident that there is a huge world-wide demand for it.

I believe a lot of this demand derives from our over-sexualised society, which is having a devastating effect on marriages, relationships, mental health and personal identity.

Within counselling, we sometimes refer to Maslow's Hierarchy of Needs.

Maslow believes that we all have basic and psychological needs that must be met in order to have self-actualisation, (also known as self-fulfilment.)

These needs do not have to be 100% achieved, but the understanding is that to reach the next level each one must be met in some way.

"[Self-actualized people] live more in the real world of nature than in the man-made mass of concepts, abstractions, expectations, beliefs and stereotypes that most people confuse with the world." - Abraham H. Maslow, Hierarchy of Needs: A Theory of Human Motivation.

I choose to mention this because today the world we live in is predominately two-dimensional.

We interact on a screen, laugh through emojis, feel jealousy when we look at people's Instagram feeds, tear up in anger at videos of injustice, speed-type our opinions, and in so doing become whoever we desire to be.

On a screen we can pretend. We don't have to be vulnerable, we don't have to be ourselves, and often we find safety in this false illusion that we have control over.

As human beings we strive after emotional connection, desiring to belong and to be loved; after all, we were not created to be alone but in community with one another.

Porn provides a hollow, fraudulent connection, and because of this has the power to isolate us.

As I have witnessed with counselling clients, pornography (or, indeed, any addiction) is not exclusively physical, but rather it permeates the whole person; body, mind and spirit.

What affects one area of our lives often impacts the rest.

What's the biggest challenge porn addicts face?

Porn users often report a cycle of guilt, where after using porn they resolve to abstain from future use, yet when they later succumb to its temptation, users experience shame, which in turn can result in isolation as they remove themselves from people around them.

This may be a result of depression or instead lead to it.

So, while porn may feel harmless and create a mere physical sensation, I urge you - don't be fooled.

Pornography leeches into and poisons your very being, significantly and adversely affecting your mental health and your ability to form healthy relationships with others.

How do you plan on raising your kids knowing what you know about this topic?

With all I have witnessed and researched around this topic I believe as a parent, one of the core principles I will implement with my children is an open environment where they can talk about anything.

Communication is key. Exposing the hidden things and bringing them into the light is essential.

However, it's important this is facilitated and nurtured in a shame-free, non-judgemental and safe environment.

What would you say to someone reading who is addicted to porn?

For anyone who is struggling with porn, I would encourage you to talk to someone you can trust; a family member, friend or pastor, and if you feel there is no one, please seek out counselling.

It's a non-judgemental and confidential environment for you to talk openly and explore your feelings, bringing the hidden things into the light.

My sincere hope and prayer is that you can be free from that which holds you captive so you can become all you can be.

— *Rebecca Hodge*

Discussion questions

1. Which principle from the wolf's code did you find most helpful?

2. Is there anything you would add to the list?

3. If so much of this advice is basic and obvious, why do you think we don't implement it in our lives?

4. What's your biggest takeaway from Rebbeca's story?

Chapter 8 - Defend The Den

Wolves are very protective of their dens. In fact, a wolf will usually only attack a human if it gets too close to the den.

(According to the movie 'The Fray' anyway.)

They take their security seriously and so should we when it comes to protecting our homes from porn.

Here are some steps you can take to make 'your territory' safe and more 'hunter proof.'

For some of you, these steps will be too overboard for others they are exactly what you need.

I'm not saying they should be things you permanently apply to your life, but they are options for you to consider and try out.

1. Get rid of the locks

We tend to find the best way to combat the hunters is to do the exact opposite of what they encourage you to do.

THE FIGHT

The best way to walk is in the reverse direction of where they are trying to lead you.

This can actually be quite a neat hack to find out what you should be doing - it's sort of like reverse engineering the hunters' traps.

For example, when Adam and Eve ate the fruit, they hid from God because of their shame rather than running to Him.

This is ironic because hiding our shortcomings is the hunters want us to do.

Many of us hide things behind locks.

Whether they are physical locks such as on a drawer/door or digital locks on phones and computers.

You see, some locks are made to keep people out while others are to keep people in.

The locks that keep people out are things like gates and the front door of your house.

They help keep you safe from harm and from unwanted visitors.

Locks that keep people in are usually defined as one thing: **a prison.**

They are designed to keep things trapped.

If we want to get serious about fighting our lust addictions, we must learn to live without locks, because more often than not they hold us prison rather than keep us safe.

Living a life of integrity doesn't mean living perfectly, rather it means accepting and being open about the fact we're not.

Locks hold secrets, they allow us to keep our dirt hidden from the world and keep up a false image of ourselves.

The hunters thrive on this 'hidden culture,' and the best way we can counteract this is by kicking the door down and shedding some light in.

In general, lust usually takes place behind locked doors, from affairs to self-gratification (for obvious reasons.)

Whether it's the bathroom, bedroom or anywhere else in between we usually develop habits and patterns around places in 'our den' (where we live or spend significant amounts of time in.)

If we're not careful, they can become a fortress that actually holds us and our secrets away from the world.

Historically it's only relatively recently that we as humans can afford the luxury of private bedrooms. A lot of you reading may still have to share a room, and in many parts of the world today most of the family still live in one room.

There's nothing wrong with having your own space (all the introverts just said amen) - but it also leads to new challenges as this book has repeatedly pointed out.

Whether you share a room or not, implementing an open door policy and removing locks will help you to tear this fortress down.

By giving your family/roommates the opportunity to walk in at a moments notice helps you tap into the power of community and accountability.

A simple way to implement this is literally just to keep the door open.

That way when the door closes someone will know something is up - including yourself. It becomes another warning sign to help you get off the train before it picks up too much speed.

The same thinking can be applied with passcodes on our phones and passwords on our laptops.

More often than not these are used to keep our secrets safe rather than 'protect us from strange unknown hackers.'

Of course, we need to be sensible here, there are legitimate reasons to have a password to protect financial and sensitive information in case your phone is stolen etc.

If that's the case, an alternative is to give your passcodes/passwords to friends and family members you trust.

In our marriage, Jaci and I have full access to each other's phones, laptops, emails and social media and have given each other liberty to go through them at any time.

This is just a small measure put in place to protect our marriage from things that would try to tear us apart.

Perhaps you would think twice about texting that guy back if you knew your wolfpack could accidentally sniff it out while on your phone.

Maybe if your dad had access to your computer to do the weekly shopping, you would be less likely to use it for porn.

Maybe not? Who knows. You won't know until you try.

Removing locks won't make you bulletproof, but it certainly helps improve accountability in your life and can act as a preventative motivation.

2. Leave your phone downstairs at night-time

This is a good habit for every member of the family.

Did you know that keeping your phone outside of your bedroom is one of the best ways to improve your sleep? That's what the science guys say anyway.

"But I need my phone for my alarm!"

No, you don't. You can get a great alarm clock for £5 - a small price to pay for better shut-eye and to get rid of those late-night temptations.

This is something that has really made a big impact on lots of different areas in my life.

You can read a wee blog I wrote about it and get the alarm clock I've found works for me at https://matthewthompson.org/blog/stop-using-phone-alarm-clock

By removing our technology (yes laptops, computers and tablet included) from our bedrooms we eliminate the issue of having the use our willpower or self-control to resist giving in.

We've changed our environment (den) to help us overcome this addiction.

This fight takes a lot of effort. Why waste it unnecessarily when we can make a small change like this?

Like removing donuts from the home if you know you're going to eat them all… it just makes sense.

3. Use technology in community

Why not make a commitment to use your tech in a community environment?

"But I need to use it for study/work! Other people distract me!"

Use headphones. Turn chair to the wall/out to the window. Go to the library.

"I can't work with music! I get distracted and sing along."

Try white noise apps, movie soundtracks AND DO whatever it takes.

You can make valid arguments against all of these suggestions, but sobriety comes at a price, and it's all down to how much you are willing to pay.

In our teens and beyond my friends and I always found that the times we struggled most were around exam time.

Whether we were triggered by the stress of exams or just plain old boredom from studying is still up for debate, but we began to highlight those study seasons as common weak points in our calendar.

Using the library or working at the kitchen table for a season is a small inconvenience to pay freedom.

Don't you think?

4. Stop taking your phone in the shower

I never got this one because I was always too feared to wreck my phone with water damage but people tell me that this became a real trigger area for them.

"But I love to listen to music in the shower!"

There are plenty of waterproof radios/speakers that you can't watch porn on - try that instead.

5. Consider downgrading your phone

For many seasons in my life, I swapped the smartphone for an old-school flip-phone… 'the brick.'

Even now I use a smartphone for work but use a basic Nokia as my personal phone so I can disconnect from the digital world when I'm not working.

Going back to basics in regards to your phone keeps you contactable while eliminating a lot of triggers like Instagram rabbit trails or questionable pop-ups.

Plus its ultra hipster right now as Nokia just re-released the 3310 (although be careful, you may get addicted to playing Snake.)

It may seem over the top or even 'impossible' in this modern age, but I think the positives outweigh the negatives.

Plus we all spend way too much time online. Cutting back on it isn't going to hurt us, in fact, it probably would really benefit us.

I find my life much simpler and richer when the phone is switched off, and the notifications go unheard.

Maybe you want to try a combo of an old phone and a tablet - whatever works for you and your legitimate needs.

(P.S. Your SnapChat story count is not a legit need.)

6. Make your body fight on your side

If you have been struggling with an addiction it is easy to feel like your body is your enemy and that's it's actively working against you rather than helping.

I know what it feels like to have nights while trying to kick the habit where you feel like you're going to explode and the only way out is to give in.

Trust me, I've been there, and it does get better.

There are a few things you can do to help retrain your body and actually use it to work for you along this journey.

7. Exercise

Did you know that exercise pumps you with the same chemicals as a hit from drugs or sexual climax?

Sweet.

One of the problems with an addict's brain is that it can no longer produce endorphins naturally without the stimulus it has become dependent on - whether it's cocaine or porn.

Exercise is a great way to get your body naturally producing again.

It's also an incredible way to release all that tension you have building up - let out frustration, anger and blow off some steam…

Plus you get to stay healthy, learn new skills and expand your Wolfpack.

(Wolfpack Wednesday workout anyone?)

Even though I work primarily as a writer and marketer, I still pick up some shifts as a bike messenger to make sure I'm using my body and getting outdoors/away from the screen.

It really does make all the difference, both to my physical and mental health.

8. Start having wet dreams

(Sorry ladies, this one is for the fellas only.)

I'll admit this one may seem a little whacky, but to be honest, this book crossed the line of being normal and PG a long time ago.

I haven't backed this up with science or anything else, it's just a theory that myself and a few friends have, so please take it with a pinch of salt.

Here we go.

Fresh sperm leads to better chances of pregnancy, so it makes sense for old sperm to be constantly ejected to make room for the new.

We reckon this could be a reason why the male body naturally encourages regular ejaculation - in a variety of forms - primarily through arousal to 'encourage you' to have sex and 'carry forward the human race.'

We think God designed a process for this to still happen even if you aren't sexually active for a season - like before marriage, travelling away from a spouse, in a season of poor health etc:

Wet dreams.

Also known as a nocturnal emission, a wet dream is when a man ejaculates in his sleep. It's our bodies way of keeping chemicals in check and 'emptying the tank' regularly.

Here's the problem: most guys I've met have never even had a wet dream because they have been taking care of 'draining the tank themselves.'

When you are sexually active, you don't have wet dreams (or as regularly) because there is no reason to... because the build up of sperm and semen is continually released manually for lack of a better term.

When a man stops regular ejaculation (whether it be masturbation or sex) it can take a while for his body to kick into the wet dream cycle.

No guy is the same, sometimes it takes weeks, sometimes it takes months, but if you stick with it they will eventually come.

In my opinion, this is an often overlooked aspect of a man's journey to freedom, but one that plays a very significant role.

Once your body retrains itself to utilise wet dreams it will really help you men out in your journey to freedom.

But by no means is it an essential or the solution to everything.

Just something to consider and look out for.

9. Cold showers

This is one has been passed down through the decades.

Some people like it, other people think it's ridiculous, and it even has become the butt of many jokes online.

("My pastor said 'just take a cold shower' now I'm just cold AND horny.")

I wasn't going to include it but figured it won't hurt.

Some people swear by taking an ice cold shower to get out of the mood FAST and quite literally cool yourself down.

Others have pointed out it's impractical and very rarely a feasible option... can't exactly just take a cold shower to the cinema, school or church.

In general, many people praise cold showers for a wide range of benefits.

You get a nice rush of chemicals, it's great for your blood flow and even good for your sleep.

Plus the marines have been using this for years because of the benefits - both mentally and physically - so why not give it a try?

It's one of those ones won't hurt so you may as well give it a go (though they are absolutely freezing.)

9. Walk away

Do a Joseph - we talked about this earlier.

Don't underestimate the power of physically walking away from a situation... it really does stop a lot of things dead in their tracks.

Whether it's getting outside, going downstairs or even just leaving a room, making a physical decision can be a quick way to stop the cycle.

Remember the later you leave it the harder it will be to leave.

10. Equip yourself with the right tools

There are some great resources out there you can use to help defend the den and keep you on track.

Use General Filters

Most internet provider will have a general 18+ filter you can put over your entire wifi network.

These can be pretty good and mean that everyone in the home using wifi will have basic protection against any explicit online sources.

A similar filter can be applied on your smartphone in the general settings.

Once set, any generic 18+ content will require a passcode that someone in your Wolfpack can set for you.

These filters don't catch everything, but they are a good first step.

Use porn specific filters

Covenant Eyes is one of the longest running internet filters out there that focuses on keeping your family safe from pornography.

They have different packages available depending on your needs.

I've also heard of people using NetNanny.

There's lots of great stuff out there, but I recommend you try them and find one that's right for you.

I think these are really important if you have children in the house.

Porn specific filters probably aren't a great option for people who are already addicted (because there will always be plenty of ways around the system.)

But they serve a really useful purpose of protecting kids from accidentally stumbling across explicit content online.

Prevention is obviously always better than a cure.

Use Accountability software

I personally recommend going down the accountability software road if you already have a problem with pornography...

The reason is that you will need to learn how to be free without simply cutting off all access to 'temptation.'

I definitely recommend implementing extreme measures for a certain period, but then you will have to start coming back to the real world eventually.

Afterall, you can't hide yourself away from people you find attractive or billboards on the street. Both will always be there, and you'll have to learn to deal with that.

There will always be ways for 'porn' or at least explicit material to make its way to you, whether it's an advertisement you drive past, a scene in a movie or a real-life scenario.

Accountability software doesn't BLOCK you from watching porn, it merely (to put it bluntly) **tells someone when you do.**

Basically, you choose someone from your Wolfpack to receive weekly updates on how what you have been up to online.

This means that someone can follow up with you and actually WALK with you on your path to freedom.

I know people who have made pastors, youth leaders or even family members their accountability partner - it definitely is a very humbling experience to go through - but they were dead serious about breaking their addiction and fair play to them because they now walk in freedom.

People I trust recommend X3 Watch and Ever Accountable.

Other tools

AdBlock: I highly recommend using an AdBlocker on whatever browser you use. There are plenty out there. Just check out the extensions on Google Chrome, Firefox etc. They really work and will stop you getting sucked onto sites you don't wanna be on or see marketing images you'd rather not.

Block Site: I use Block Site on Chrome to stop me from checking social media when working. It's really easy to use and can act as another hurdle for you to overcome if you are trying to engage in a habit you're trying to kick. Whether it's Facebook, YouTube or your favourite porn website.

11. Support groups

Online support groups are no substitute for your real-life wolf pack, but they can be a way to keep you and your pack inspired to keep on going and expose you to new resources, tips/tricks and SUCCESS stories.

There's the NoFap community on Reddit and some online groups via XXX Church. But hey, you could always start your own.

12. Put your money where your mouth is

I get it, we are all young and trust me I know money is tight. I know what it's like to be a teenager when it comes to money.

I also know how quick we are to spend money on pointless things and I do believe in the power of putting our money where our mouths are.

We often commit to things more when more of us are committed to them - by committing our money we put more on the line to follow something through.

Let me make this very clear, no resource will ever be the ultimate answer or your magic bullet, but they may be tools to help you along your way.

Some people having great success with courses and software, others don't.

I've heard of some groups setting up the lust equivalent of a 'swear jar' so that they take a financial hit every time they watch porn or masturbate, but again you have to find something that will work for you.

In my opinion, the best thing you could invest your money in is some form of counselling or therapy. If you are in a position where you can access that (even free opportunities) then please take them.

Every time I read over this chapter I feel a little underwhelmed. I feel like there should be more I can offer you guys but honestly, so much of this fight is in the emotional, mental and spiritual parts of us rather than the physical.

For me, the most beneficial physical changes you can make are

to your home environment to help manage your digital diet.

Do all you can to make it one that is healthy + liberating.

In the next chapter, we're going to discuss one of the most important yet essential ingredients in our fight for freedom. It's the glue that holds all of this together and I've already mentioned it multiple times throughout the book.

The Wolfpack.

STORIES FROM THE WOLFPACK
- Julie Patterson: Social Worker

Who Are You?

My name is Julie Patterson, I'm a 45-year-old happily married mother of three (with one of my lovely children being Matthew!)

Professionally I've spent a large part of my career working as a Social Worker with adolescents and consider this one of my biggest joys in life.

What impact do you think lust/porn is having on society?

Growing up in the 1970s and 1980s I had little knowledge of and absolutely no exposure to pornography.

In this era, porn was only available on the top shelf in newsagents. However now with the ease of access to the internet, it is readily available on mobile phones and can be therefore be viewed in any place at any time.

In my view, porn depicts women in a very false and unnatural manner. Real-life females are not like those who can be viewed in porn, that are airbrushed, have had implants and are groomed within an inch of their lives.

These women who star in such movies have no bumps or lumps, no stretch marks and bear little resemblance to the average female body. Plus these women always are "up for it," never are too tired or just not in the mood.

I believe therefore that watching porn may give young guys the wrong impression of women and has the potential to leave them disappointed when they enter into a relationship with someone who is after all human rather than a sex symbol on a screen.

It seems likely that porn may give people the impression that sex is something to be taken and demanded if and when they want it. It fails to outline the issue of consent and does nothing to show sex in the context of a loving marriage.

This may lead young men to treat their wives in a way which is not loving or respectful which has the potential to ultimately destroy the relationship.

I'm also aware that the number of women consuming porn is massive. It would be heartbreaking to think that these young women think what they see on screen is normal.

It is not and is usually considered abusive in the real-world.

How did you feel when Matthew first told you about his porn problem?

I first found out that Matthew had an addiction to porn when he confessed it on Facebook.

To say I was shocked would be an understatement. Matthew was always a quiet 'Christian boy' and I had no idea that viewing porn would even be something he would consider.

Regrettably, I asked Matthew to take down his post because I was embarrassed.

As the years went by we chatted about it and it was only recently when I read a draft of his book that I realised the full impact this had on his life... I would be lying if I said I really understand how someone could be addicted to pornography but I do know for Matthew and others that this is a real issue.

What advice would you give to parents in regards to this issue?

The thought that one of my children may be viewing porn honestly never entered my head.

As a bit of a worrier by nature, I had loads of concerns about my children, but porn didn't factor into the equation.

I never activated any safeguards or parental controls on the internet, simply because I didn't know they were needed.

That may seem naive on my part, but you must understand that during Matthew's childhood, computers and the internet were only being introduced into the home (for the first time in history.)

We were the first generation of parents to walk through this big change in our society... and of course, we didn't always get it right (something that spans across all the generations!)

My advice to parents now is to use whatever controls are available to prevent your children gaining access to pornography. The internet is a positive thing, but it is also a portal that enables your children to access all kinds of harmful content.

Put on the parental controls, check your child's browsing history and have an open door policy when they are accessing the internet.

More importantly though, be open to the possibility that your innocent little angels may well be viewing porn and developing an addiction which can be difficult to break and can have an impact on their future relationships.

Talk to your children about this issue. Be open, don't get mad or judge them and most of all walk alongside your children to try to help them overcome.

What would you say to kids who are afraid to tell their parents?

For any young person struggling with pornography, my advice would be to tell at least one of your parents.

They may well be shocked as maybe like me they didn't know porn was such a big issue or such a struggle for young people today.

But even if they are shocked and tell you off, or shout…they will calm down (sometimes even parents say things without really thinking!) Most parents generally really love their children and want to understand them so they can to help.

Parents don't want their children to be struggling with something on their own or to be carrying a lot of shame and guilt.

Even parents have made mistakes so they are likely to be more understanding that you may think.

So talk to your parents, share your issue and give them this book to read. It may help explain things better than you can.

Confiding in a parent means they can help you with strategies to help you stop accessing porn.

They can hold you accountable and will support you, cheering you on each step of the way.

- *Julie Patterson*

Discussion questions

1. Which tactic stood out to you the most?

2. What would you add to this list?

3. What practical measures are you going to implement this week?

4. What's your biggest takeaway from Julie's story?

Chapter 9 - Assemble A Wolfpack

"If you want to go quickly go alone.
If you want to go far, go together"
- African Proverb

Let me tell you a story about a situation one of my friends found himself in.

At the time he was living in a walled compound in a Kenyan Village. To set the scene think of big walls, spikes and a single gate to let cars in and out.

They had lots of guard dogs - a whole pack of them - for protection. This guy thought it was odd but ruled it out as just a culture thing.

The dogs weren't particularly fierce looking, but there were a lot of them.

One morning he woke up to some commotion outside.

The people in the compound were chatting excitedly - it was way too early, and my friend was kinda cranky - but he got up to see what all the fuss was about.

Let's just say his jaw hit the deck when he got outside because in the courtyard lay a dead lion.

WHAT?!

Turns out a lioness had made her way into the compound, and the dogs took her out.

To this day I still contest this story. In my head, there is no way that a bunch of dogs could take our the king of the jungle (or in this case the 'Queen' I suppose,) but regardless it acts as a pretty cool metaphor for the power of a pack.

Another great example is how wolves hunt in packs. Wolves can easily take out animals that are HUGE in comparison to the pups, but by working together, they can enjoy a real feast.

In this chapter, I'm going to show you why forming a Wolfpack is essential in taking down the hunters and mastering lust in your life.

For some, this could be the hardest part of this journey, but you guys came here for a challenge right?

Don't be a lone wolf

A wolf isolated from the pack has the highest chance of being hunted and killed.

It's the same with us humans too. When we are isolated, we are vulnerable.

Remember how we talked about the fact that we are made for community?

How God said: *'it's not good for man to be alone?'*

That's because we are strongest when we are together.

We are strongest in a Wolfpack .

The problem

Our western culture is more individualistic than ever before. We don't like to show our weaknesses, so we isolate ourselves and become lone wolves.

Infact, the lone wolf is a celebrated figure in in our culture.

Think about how many of the big flicks are focused on ONE individual who takes on the world, kills a million bad guys and overcomes impossible, incredible obstacles.

Well in the real world the bad guys don't have such a terrible aim or freeze up when we try to attack them…

They shoot to kill and don't hold anything back.

The lone wolf is fictional. In the real world, the lone wolf doesn't survive.

What is the function of a Wolfpack?

A Wolfpack works together towards the same goal.

For wolves that means defending the den and hunting for food to survive.

For us, that means overcoming challenges, exposing blind spots and tackling problems as a pack.

A strong Wolfpack of friends allows you to go far and to go together.

It binds you together and helps you overcome whatever life throws at you together,

You know that your pack has your back covered and they know you have theirs.

Here are some of the key areas of impact my Wolfpack has had in my life.

1. Expose blind spots

Having a Wolfpack means that there are more eyes on your life than just your own.

This means that people can pick up on your blind spots and weak areas in your life.

The things you can't see about yourself: habits, traits or things you do to self-sabotage yourself. These things can be called out and identified by your pack to help you overcome them.

A Wolfpack continually checks up on you, keeping you accountable to the commitment you've made to fight against lust.

It's a place to open up, be vulnerable and shine light on the areas of your life the hunters want to keep in darkness and hold us hostage.

A Wolfpack does all this with love. Not with a critical mind or judgemental eye - but with a humility that says *'I'm no better'* - and heart that says *'we're in this fight together.'*

2. Celebrate in victory, encourage in defeat

There's a reason why teams are so important in sport.

One of the best feelings of scoring an incredible goal is celebrating with your squad.

One of the most encouraging feelings when you miss is that fistbump from a teammate who lets you know, *'don't worry dude, you'll get it next time.'*

A Wolfpack will stick by you in the good and the bad, they won't judge you for messing up.

It's an awesome thing to celebrate your wins along your journey. I remember each of us hitting certain milestones and celebrating with each other.

("ONE MONTH FREE YEAHHH BOIII!")

But there were also times we messed up, broke a solid win streak and had to start again. It was in those times the Wolfpack tapped into its true potential.

To be encouraged, rallied around and cheered on helps keep you going when things get tough.

That's the role of the Wolfpack.

3. Have fun

Plain and simple.

Having a Wolfpack and doing life together is absolutely legendary and a lot of fun.

The Little Red Car: How Our Wolfpack Started

Forming a Wolfpack was the game changer in my own journey.

My buddy Steve had just learnt how to drive and got a car… a sweet red Fiat Punto Grande (one of the most European cars you can imagine.)

He was 17, I was 16.

It was Steve that actually invited me to go to Germany where I first heard the tale of the wolf.

We weren't even that close. We knew each other through rugby and Maths class, but one day he leaned over and was like *"hey you wanna go to Germany? I think it would be cool."*

So we went, and our lives changed forever.

After coming back from mainland Europe, we would hang out in his awesome wee car and drive around either chasing after love or fast food (the two are often one.)

I never really talked about any serious 'deep' personal stuff with anyone before then. I had loads of mates, but we were too cool to be weak. All that changed with one simple question one night in the McDonalds car park.

"Hey man, is there anything you want prayer for before you go?"

This simple question radically changed our friendship group as teens.

We started asking this any time someone got out of the car at the end a night out. It became part of our circle's culture, and from that a Wolfpack was born.

People shared about pornography addictions, depression, family issues, health issues, same sex-attraction, dreams, fear, anxieties, passions, goals - you name it.

It transformed our squad from 'hi-bye' casual friendships to deep, meaningful, life-giving relationships. The crazy thing is we were all between 15 and 18 years old.

Steve was the best man at our wedding two years ago. He roasted me in his speech (I had plenty of embarrassing stories for him to pull from) and is still a crucial part of my Wolfpack all these years later.

All because of a question asked in a little red car (which I actually drive now haha.)

All it took was that first step. A question that took things a little bit deeper.

Taking the first step.

Enter commonly circulated sweeping statement: They say men aren't as good as women when it comes to opening up with each other and sharing the messy heart stuff.

The media portrays it as uncool for guys to open up with each other. That it is feeble and a sign of weakness.

This is a pile of wolf-crap and it's destroying men's lives.

At the extreme end, you have the fact that suicide rates are up to 3 times higher amongst men.

At the other end of the spectrum, you have the fact that guys are walking around without anyone calling out their blind spots.

Quite frankly this leads to guys becoming insecure jerks and stunts us from growing into our full potential as men.

Being a lone wolf is clearly not working for us, so we have got to get over this proud desire to be tough and our fear of being seen as weak.

I have lost male friends to suicide and have battled it myself.

Nothing stings like it, and I know the hardest thing to do sometimes is to open your mouth.

But no matter who you are reading this book (male or female, young or old) you need to nail this area of your life, and you need to do it now.

We must learn how to be vulnerable in a trusted community of people who care about us. When we do, we become much more equipped to tackle whatever life throws at us.

The lone wolf model doesn't work.

Taking the first step can be hard, but it's one you must take.

Who's in a Wolfpack?

I'm a big believer that your Wolfpack should be made up of the same sex as you - not because I'm trying to push some sort of an agenda - but just because from my experience I found the following:

- I don't want to share my deep dark secrets about pornography with a girl I thought was cute (because of my pride.)

- There are some differences between how men and women experience life especially when it comes to sexuality (see how many men read 50 Shades Of Grey vs how many women do.)

- I became attracted to any girl I got emotionally close to as a teen.

Maybe you guys are more superior human beings than me, but this is certainly what I found (and I did try both options.)

I can't decide what's best for you guys so ultimately it's up to you, but at its core, a Wolfpack should be a group of friends who you love, can be open with and trust.

It doesn't matter if it starts with one friend or a whole group… usually, once you get the conversation going with one person, it filters into the rest of the circle.

A note on parents

This can be very tricky but has the potential to be very worth-while.

I failed in this area because of fear. I wish I had of taken the step in my teens because looking back I know it would have been a game-changer.

My secret distanced me from my family… even though they did nothing wrong. So now I'm urging you not to make the same mistake I did.

I don't know any of your family backgrounds, but I do suggest where appropriate to bring your parent(s) or parental figure in on this issue.

Don't be afraid to give them this book to help them understand. Remember it can be hard for them to process because they most likely grew up in a different culture.

I think having a loving, supportive parent on board could be a really beneficial thing.

Yes it's awkward, yes it's some tough conversations to have, but some parents do want to be involved in their teenager's lives and many are sad that they aren't because we tend to shut them out.

Again this is your call, you know your family situation far better than I do and you know what decision makes sense for you.

What holds us back?

Put simply I think the biggest things that hold us back are the lies from the hunters:

'You're the only one with this problem.'
'Your friends will think you're a huge creep.'
'You're going to get cut off and become the topic of gossip/scandal.'

Here's the truth:

- If people don't want or can't handle the real you with all your hang-ups and weaknesses then they certainly aren't the type of people you want to call as friends and you don't want them sticking around. BYE FELICIA. I've got no time for people who expect perfection from me because I will never be able to offer it to them.

- Society has become so liberal about issues of sexuality that your friends probably won't bat an eyelid because it has become so normalised.

- The statistics make the most probable response to be the following:

ME TOO.

These two words are probably the most potent and powerful combination of letters in the English language because they shatter the lies of the hunters.

Even if it's not a 'full blown' pornography addiction, we're still all sexual people.

It's likely they will have some sort of lust going on that they're trying to figure out.

But here's the thing… It takes someone to make that first step.

It takes a bold, courageous trailblazer to get the conversation going that will give birth to a Wolfpack.

That person is you.

"No no, not me, I can't!"

You can and you must, because if you don't no one else will.

Sure, it's incredibly daunting to put your cards on the table because of the taboo and all the other stuff.

But someone has to do it to get the ball rolling.

How to initiate a Wolfpack

Here are a few ideas:

- **Post an article on social media** or send it to a group of friends and see what the response is "hey man, what do you think about this article?" This could be a good way to get the conversation going without you having to fumble your way onto the topic yourself.

- **Send this book to some friends.** I don't mind being the one to break the ice, that's why I am writing this book so that I can at least get the conversation going for some people. *"Hey, curious to hear your thoughts about what this crazy guy from Northern Ireland wrote about."*

- **Start having intentional conversations with your friends.** This starts with moving away from the trivial stuff and focusing on things that matter. *"How's your family? What's going on in your life? Everything alright? Anything I can help you out with? Anything I can pray for?"* The deeper you go, the easier it is to share things.

- **Just come out and say it**. Choose your moment with a friend you trust: *"Look I know this might sound weird, but I'm trying to stop watching porn because I've read up about what the side effects can be and I was wondering if could keep me accountable?*

How to move forward with your pack

Meet regularly:
Your wolfpack should be people you see regularly. Not just once a year, preferably people you are in close community with, live life together with and spend time together once a week.

Get the conversation going:
This book deals with a wide spectrum of stuff, not all of which you have to agree with. It could, however, be a good way to power through some issues and get the ball rolling. There are discussion questions at the end of each chapter to get you started. Use them to study, debate and wrestle with each other.

Pray together:
Don't underestimate the power of prayer and especially the power

of prayer in community. It's a powerful way to get closer, rally behind each other and see some great answers and victories.

Establish a judgement-free zone:
Set a culture where no one is judged no matter what they share. Remember we are all just as guilty as each other, we all have fallen short. We all are in the same boat, therefore, none of us has the right to judge.

Stay humble:
Let's say you start to see some serious progress, you're 2 months 'sober' but some of your friends can't make it past 3 days. HEY DUDE/DUDETTE don't be a jerk about it. This isn't a competition. You have no right to boast
or put yourself above anyone because just a few weeks ago you were in the exact same position.

Check-in online:
Whatsapp groups, Facebook groups, IG DM groups. Whatever the cool kids are using these days, it's a great way to ping a wee message when you're struggling or need some encouragement. (You could also pick up the phone or meet up #oldschool.)

Have fun:
This isn't about getting a pity party together. This is a journey - an adventure - that you get to walk out with a group of friends. Have fun along the way, create great memories together: work out, hike, go on vacation with your Wolfpack. You really do only get your youth once. Squeeze everything you can out of it.

Your Wolfpack is an essential part of overcoming this addiction and will set you up in a solid position for just about anything life throws at you. Don't neglect it. Don't be a lone wolf.

We are stronger together.

We are stronger as a pack.

"For the strength of the Pack is the Wolf, and the strength of the Wolf is the Pack." - From the Jungle Book by Rudyard Kipling.

These three elements of THE FIGHT are essential.

One cannot exist without the other.

Don't be afraid to experiment and come up with other tactics you can apply to help you in this journey.

This book doesn't contain all the answers. A lot of them are for you to discover yourself.

As I've mentioned repeatedly, my faith has been foundational in my journey to freedom.

But I also promised that I would respect you if you come from a different faith or background.

I wanted this book to be accessible and beneficial for everyone, not just Christians.

The next section of the book is all about God and how I see him playing into all of this.

If that's not for you, then go ahead and skip to the last section of the book VICTORY.

Though you may be interested to see how this piece of the puzzle brings it all together...

STORIES FROM THE WOLFPACK
- Stephen Hinds: Mechanical Engineer

Who are you?

My name is Stephen Hinds; I'm a close friend of Matthew and part of the same awesome wolfpack of mates!

Tell us a wee bit about your journey with lust

My journey with lust began at the age of 10.

I had a friend at the time who was a bit older than me, and he told me about this thing called masturbation (lol.)

I had absolutely no idea what he was talking about, but it didn't take me long to work it out and try it for myself. I hadn't hit puberty at the time and didn't even know what sex was.

Once I began high school, I was introduced to porn. My hormonal, confused teenage mind soon became totally hooked. It affected me more than I could ever have thought.

I grew up in the church, but they, like many churches and youth groups, failed to educate us on this issue.

It was a topic nobody wanted to address, but to be fair at that time no one really knew just how accessible porn was and how much of a problem it was for us.

People were sharing images and videos around school like popcorn, and it was completely normal for the group I was hanging around with at the time.

My family knew nothing. I was living a secret life worlds apart from the life they thought I was living.

I couldn't look at girls the same, and I viewed them as objects to be consumed.

Everywhere I looked, I was seeing the images back in my head of the videos I had viewed earlier that day, and every girl I looked at was compared to these unrealistic, fictional women.

What changed?

This addiction lasted for a few years, but thankfully God brought Matt into my life.

Matthew and I had similar struggles and we became great friends very quickly. We went to Germany when were 16 and that's where we first heard the story of the wolf which this whole book is built around.

God began to do some amazing things in our lives, through camps, church, and bringing some brilliant, godly people into our lives. We soon had a great group of male friends around us who were in the same boat.

These were guys we could trust.
They were our wolfpack.

We decided amongst ourselves that we were going to fight this battle head-on. Being guys all of a similar age, facing the same problems, we knew that we could help and encourage each other through the fight.

It took us to be vulnerable with each other and to fully trust in God to help us figure it out, because frankly we had all tried and failed on our own so many times before.

Late nights together led to many prayers and encouragements, and gradually, we began to see breakthrough in our fights. Little hourly, daily, weekly victories began to take place in our lives as we stood and fought together.

What does Victory look like to you?

Victory for me came when after many failed attempts, I began to see change in the way I was thinking.

I no longer wanted to look at those images.
I no longer needed to get off every night just to fall asleep.
I no longer viewed girls as objects and began to look past their physical features.

God had broken the chains that had bound me for so long. There were still temptations, don't get me wrong, but I had a new perspective and the strength to fight that I had never experienced before.

I knew this strength had completely come from God, as it was as though someone had flicked a switch on my life.

I felt like a totally new person.

If it weren't for my Wolfpack, I would never have had the encouragement to start, or have the essential support network I needed when I fell.

The Wolfpack was crucial to my fight against lust, and that same group of friends still forms a crucial part of my walk with God today, 7 years later.

It's hilarious to see all of us starting to get married and 'grow-up.' When we hang out, it just feels like it always did and we've kept that culture of honesty, vulnerability and openness.

I'm getting married myself next year and am so grateful to have dealt with this addiction before I entered into that.

What would you say to encourage the 16 year old version of yourself?

If I were to go back in time and speak to a younger version of myself still caught in the chains of lust, I would say to get a group of godly friends in your life that you can trust.

People you know won't judge you and are prepared to pray and fight for you.

For the men reading this in particular, I would also say that it's OK for guys to be vulnerable with other guys.

It takes far more guts to be honest and real with each other than it does to withhold your struggles.

One last thing… The chains that bind us are really only threads and threads are easily broken.

— *Stephen Hinds*

Discussion question

1. Write down people in your life who you can talk to about these issues.

2. How are you going to start a Wolfpack or go deeper with the one you currently have?

3. What are the obstacles holding you back from being open with your parents, friends, or other people in your life? How do you plan to overcome them?

4. What's your biggest takeaway from Steve's story?

THE ALPHA

Chapter 10 - Who is the Alpha?

"Aslan is a lion- the Lion, the great Lion." "Ooh" said Susan. "I'd thought he was a man. Is he-quite safe? I shall feel rather nervous about meeting a lion"... "Safe?" said Mr Beaver ... "Who said anything about safe? 'Course he isn't safe. But he's good. He's the King, I tell you." - C.S Lewis

Every Wolfpack has a leader called 'the Alpha.'

Culture has grasped onto this idea and ran with it using the term to describe someone who is the dominant force in a group or the natural leader...

Asides from all of this, 'Alpha' is actually the first letter in the greek ALPHAbet (I honestly just made that connection while typing this lol.)

I'm stealing this concept straight from the last book of the Bible because it works surprisingly well with the wolf metaphor.

"I am the Alpha and Omega, the beginning and the end." - Revelation 22:13

This verse is a quote from God himself. He's basically saying:

I am the A to Z and everything in between (no it's not Amazon...) I started this, and I'm going to be the one to finish it.
It's his final war speech just after he defeats the enemy for good, sealing the deal and delivering the final blow that leads to victory.

Remember how Adam rebelled against God and caused this mess in the first place? (Cut him some slack, if he didn't I certainly would have.)

Well, the Alpha is the leader because he has proven himself more capable than all the others in the pack.

God didn't simply abandon humanity, even when we spat in his face.

Today he still doesn't abandon us, even when we are in our darkest moments.

Even when we are 3 videos in, he is still beside us, still ready and willing to fight for us and still full of love.

He is the epitome of a good Father and will do anything for his kids.

What happened?

As soon as Adam blew it in Eden, God delivered an ultimatum to the enemy and hope for humanity in one sentence.

"He {the enemy} will strive your heel, but you {humanity} will crush his head." - Genesis 3:15

Paraphrase: *'Look Adam, you and all the future generations are going to be battling this enemy for a very long time, but don't worry,*

I already have a plan, a secret weapon... the champion of heaven who will put this snake back in its place and defeat him once and for all.'

The Lion Of Judah

From Aslan in *The Chronicles of Narnia* to Mufasa in *The Lion King*, lions have always been used as a symbol of power and leadership…

"They are king of the jungle after all."

In THE HUNTER section, we discussed how Peter says the enemy "prowls around like a roaring lion, looking for someone to devour."

One of my friends told me something really interesting one time about roaring lions and this verse.

Allegedly the only time a lion roams around by itself and roars is when it's frightened and cut off from the pride (a pack of lions.)

This gave me a whole new perspective on this verse.

How the enemy is actually isolated and vulnerable. Still dangerous absolutely - I for one wouldn't like to meet a lion even if it was scared and by itself…

But this is especially interesting when we read one of the nicknames for the champion of heaven:

'The Lion Of Judah.'

Read that Peter verse again:

"Stay alert! Watch out for your great enemy, the devil. He prowls

around like a roaring lion, looking for someone to devour."

Here we see that the enemy is only **LIKE** a lion. A false imitation of something powerful.

In some ways, porn is also **LIKE** a lion.

It's presented as being strong, masculine and dominant - '**LIKE a lion**' - but in the end, it leads to weakness, emasculation and bondage.

Porn falsely promises strength and courage.

Porn is easy, on-demand, non-committal, selfish and requires no vulnerability or effort.

Similiarly, the enemy is false and hollow.

This simply isn't the case for the champion of heaven.

He **is** the Lion of Judah. He **is** the real deal. He **is** strong, powerful and deadly.

"Okay okay, stop stalling. Who is this champion of heaven?"

Chances are you've already heard of him.

His name is Jesus.

STORIES FROM THE WOLFPACK
- Rob Rass: Aid-Worker

Who are you?

My name is Rob Rass. I currently work as an aid worker supporting humanitarian efforts in conflict zones (currently in South Sudan.)

This job takes me into some pretty dark places but also teaches me so much about God's scandalous love for us despite our mess, transforming our ashes into beauty.

I first met Matt in Rwanda where we lived and worked together for 3 months!

What impact do you think porn is having outside of the western world?

It is not easy to understand the impact of porn because it's even more submerged and secretive than in the west. Like the tip of an iceberg, we only see the issue occasionally addressed at the surface level.

The impact is unknown, and I've not heard it talked about in African churches. This imposes a cultural silence on the issue and its effects. Contrary to what you might think, a huge amount of the African population has a smartphone, especially the youth. They in particular are super-stoked about tech and like to follow the latest trends.

However, underneath this iceberg, the rest of society is not talking with this young generation about porn, often instead invoking stigma or just silence, keeping a vicious iceberg submerged.

How well do international churches deal with the issue?

In many international churches, there are pastors, ministers and priests who are held up to be shining examples of holiness and purity. This is a good thing when founded on real values lived out by leaders of the church. However, if the church just expects their leaders to be pure and holy, without creating a platform to be vulnerable and speak on issues of porn, it causes dysfunction in the church.

Topics such as healthy relationships seem to be on the rise, especially amongst youth groups, but the impact of porn can only be dealt with when a whole church body seeks purity together and not just expecting their pastor to keep up appearances.

What's the best thing you've done for your purity?

One of the best things I have done is what I call turning off the noise. This is needed because we experience so much distraction, advertisements and media that silently plant thoughts in our minds.

I found breakthrough when I became intentional about my thought life, choosing to turn off the noise through ending my day with seven minutes of silence.

Even though it is a hard thing to do, it's worthwhile and leads to deeper prayer life, enabling more love and light to take their rightful place in our search for purity.

— *Rob Rass*

Discussion questions

1. Who do you think Jesus is? Set aside everything you've been told and what the people around you say (whether it's good or bad.) Who you YOU think he is?

2. What's your biggest takeaway from Rob's story?

Chapter 11 - Why is he the top dog?

"For God so loved the world, that he sent his only son. That whoso-ever believes in him shall not perish but will have everlasting life"
- John 3:16

This is probably the most quoted verse in the whole Bible and for a good reason, because it provides a clear mission statement for Jesus.

1. He is the son of God.
2. He was sent into the world to unite God and the world.
3. He was sent because God loves the world.
4. He was sent to put right what Adam made wrong.

I'm going to attempt to cram a lot of info in a small space here, but you're a smart cookie, and I know you can keep up.

Hopefully, it will answer a lot of the questions you may have about Jesus.

"Why did we need Jesus in the first place?"

Put simply: because God is holy…. That's a small word that means a whole lot of things.

If something is holy, it means that nothing unholy can come near it. Think about a bright light, even if you surround it with darkness the area around it is still filled with light.

A lot of people see holiness as something timid that can be easily smudged or tarnished like a white bed sheet. Well, I think the opposite is true.

I think holiness is incredibly powerful and anything unholy is utterly consumed by pure unadulterated holiness.

Thanks to our rebellion instigated by the enemy we are now unholy and cut off from God.

This meant that after Adam we couldn't approach God. Despite his love for us, we were separated from God (by our own doing, remember that.)

The Old Testament had some pretty tough times, a world without light and without hope. But God promised throughout it that he would send someone to save the world, someone to change everything…

Enter Jesus

The only problem was, things didn't quite go as people expected.

The biggest let down In history*

*so it seemed.

Being born to a virgin in a manky cave in Bethlehem (literally the middle of nowhere,) escaping a massacre and fleeing to Egypt to stay alive was hardly the welcome people had expected 'the chosen one' to receive.

But don't worry, it only gets worse.

For 30 years Jesus grew up in a deadbeat town and became a carpenter.

A CARPENTER. Let's just say the hype was well and truly gone about this guy. Until Jesus' cousin shows up.

Enter John the Baptist

A beast of a man who had one of the largest followings in the nation at that time and was respected as someone who heard from God (a prophet.)

He was rocking the boat of the religious world - who like some religious circles today put God in a box and use religion as a means to rule over people and gain power/wealth for themselves.

Can you imagine how they felt when John publicly endorsed Jesus as the son of God, and a voice from heaven backed it up?

It was time. After laying low his whole life, Jesus began to execute the mission he was sent to complete.

Walking on water, healing the sick, raising people from the dead and even resisting a deal from the devil himself... let's just say people began to take notice.

Miracle after miracle he blew people away, and when he spoke they knew they had found the light they were waiting for all these years.

But the religious leaders knew this would be the end of them, and it wasn't long before the enemy started scheming with them (and one of Jesus' mates Judas) to try and take this champion down.

Jesus became #1 on the enemy's hit list, and he wasn't going to rest until heaven's champion lay dead.

To people's disbelief, he succeeded.

Within 3 years Jesus lay dead in an unmarked grave, his following completely scattered and people once again without hope.

His mother and friends - who were promised so much - watched him be slowly tortured to death on a cross.

The people thought he would be their king, set them free from the slavery of the Romans and lead Israel back into its glory days.

But instead, this carpenter was nailed to two planks of wood under a mocking sign that read: 'here hangs Jesus, the so-called 'king of the Jews.'

The enemy had succeeded, Jesus was assassinated, and all hope was lost.

Briefly.

The biggest plot twist in history

You see the Alpha had a master plan. One that he constructed way back before the beginning of time when he knew Adam was going to mess up.

He was always one step ahead of the game and already had a checkmate lined up before he started playing... bizarrely, that checkmate was the death of his son on the cross.

You see, Jesus knew becoming king of Israel wouldn't be enough to save humanity, even though the people wanted him to (they even tried to force him to be king at one point.)

He knew the only option was for him to bridge the gap between God and humanity, between holiness and unholiness, between darkness and light - not just for the people alive at the time - but for everyone.

He saw the big picture.

As we said, holiness cannot mix with unholiness. It consumes and destroys it immediately.

Newton's Third Law states: *for every action, there is an equal and opposite reaction.*

You see, there is a consequence for everything - it's a law of the universe.

Our sin (rebellion against God) does not come without a consequence.
You wouldn't be reading a book about pornography if this wasn't true.

Mankind has racked up a bill of unholiness that we can't pay.

Jesus lived a sinless life, but he faced the same struggles you and I do. He would have been tempted by lust and every other temptation out there.

But he never gave in.

When Jesus strapped himself onto the cross (because if he really were who he claimed to be, he would have had the power to get down at any point) he was presenting himself a sacrifice - a spiritual, blameless sacrifice without sin.

In that moment God laid on him the full punishment of the world's debt. Jesus took on the debt and paid the price in full.

We are told that the suffering Jesus went through was so severe that God himself had to turn his face away.

Think about that for a second.

The punishment for the world's evil was unleashed upon this blameless champion of heaven and that it was so extreme that **the creator of the universe had to look away.**

Jesus held on until his mission was complete before saying some of the most poignant words in history:

"It is finished."

Mission Accomplished

I can imagine the enemy throwing a massive party after this, celebrating his victory.

Heaven's champion hung dead on a tree, and he had finally got one over on the big man upstairs.

All his scheming and planning had finally worked out.

But then, a knock on the door.

Don't think he would have been too happy to see who it was.

Guess who's back?

"Hey Lu, sorry to ruin your party, just need to grab these* from you."

202

(*These being the keys to death and the grave.)

Imagine the enemy's cry of disbelief when he realised he has been played.

That just as he thought victory belonged to him a swift checkmate was dealt.

3 days later Jesus physically rose from the dead to prove he had overcome death itself and give his Wolfpack their own mission before ascending to his rightfully earned seat in heaven beside God the Father.

The rest, as they say, is history.

That's why he's the leader of the pack

That's why he's the Alpha. Because no one has ever done something like that before and no one will ever do it again.

He made the ultimate sacrifice and paid the highest price for his pack.

I think that earns him the right to be the leader of the pack…

Don't you?

STORIES FROM THE WOLFPACK
- Brad Reed: Pastor of NYC Dream Center

Who are you?

I'm Brad Reed, a 30-something-year-old living in Manhattan and a pastor at the NYC Dream Center.

Along with my wife Stella and our four kids, we've committed our lives to serving people right where they are to where God dreams for them to be.

Do pastors struggle with this too?

There is an unspoken assumption that spiritual leaders are somehow above temptation and fleshly weaknesses.

Because of this assumption, pastors not only struggle with lust and temptation but usually have no outlet to process and get help.

This gap creates a spiritual mask that pastors are extremely tempted to wear.

How would you encourage someone in your church who is too afraid to open up about their addiction?

You are only as sick as your secrets.

Fear causes us to hide, and shame causes us to cover up.

Real ministry always happens in the light.

The short-term pain of humbling ourselves is far less painful than the years of pain and suffering hidden sin causes us in our lives.

What do you think is the most important thing the Church can do going forward with this issue?

The church must get a new revelation on integrity.

Integrity is about being falseless, not faultless.

As pastors, we must lead the charge and create cultures where the picture of the perfect Christian gets shattered for the reality of broken people who desperately need the saving grace of Jesus Christ.

We must understand that sin has caused all the areas of our lives to be broken and only God can bring the peace we have been longing for in our lives.

- Brad Reed

Discussion questions

1. How does reading about what Jesus did make you feel?

2. What's your biggest takeaway from Brad's story?

Chapter 12 - The Promises For His Pack

"The thief [the enemy] comes to seek, kill and destroy, but I [the Alpha] have come to give you life and life more abundantly" - John 10:10

Not just life, but a full and abundant life, one where you are free from addiction and free to pursue the good plans and missions the Alpha has for you.

When I decided to write this book I wanted to be as honest and open as possible.

I mean if you're going to write about pornography and be labelled publicly as the 'porn guy' you may as well go the whole distance.

Many people suggested this book would be more successful if it wasn't from a Christian perspective and was more 'secular' or 'scholarly.'

Maybe they would be right, but I know for a fact I would be doing you guys a disservice and not being true to my own story.

That being said… Here's my complete honest opinion:

We don't have a porn problem. We have a sin problem.

For me, without addressing the sin issue, all this book would do is attempt to treat a symptom.

Let me make this very clear: you can absolutely break an addiction without prayer, religion and faith - I've seen loads of people do it - but in my opinion, you only deal with a symptom rather than the root.

Only Jesus can address the core of our pain. He and he alone is the answer to humanity's brokenness.

Here's the deal, I'm not going to force you into anything because honestly, I can't. Free will is the most precious thing you have, and it's your choice how you spend it.

Living out a life with Jesus isn't easy, I'm not even going to pretend that it is.

In the Bible, Jesus himself tells us to count the cost before we commit our lives to him.

It takes guts, and it takes sacrifice - not just a little - but everything you've got.

His own life on earth should be proof enough that a life of faith is far from the health, wealth and prosperity some preachers will try to offer you.

But it's an invitation - an opportunity - to take back your freedom and take back this world from the hunters who know that even now it is slipping away from them.

I met Jesus in the middle of the darkest season of my life.

He traded my addictions, suicidal thoughts and brokenness in exchange for a full, purpose-driven life.

It has been far from easy, but no matter what way I run the numbers or count the cost it comes out worthy every single time. This is what's on the line, and it's yours for the taking, but it's something only you can do yourself.

The Bible tells us to join the Alpha's Wolfpack all we have to do is recognise him as number 1 (as Lord of everything,) confess that we can't do it ourselves and give our lives to him.

Take a few minutes to decide what you really wanna do.

I've tried to lay it all out for you in the best way I know how. The rest is up to you.

If it's not for you that's fine, it's your decision, and the last section of the book is there waiting for you.

But if it is something you wanna do there's a prayer below to guide you in making a commitment.

It's not just about repeating it word for word, rather it's about making a genuine pact with Jesus in your own way.

The words below are really more there to guide you if you need them.

If you've already prayed a prayer like this before, or identify as a Christian, go ahead and pray it again. Use it as an opportunity to recommit yourself to Jesus and ask for his help and healing in your life. It certainly won't hurt.

"Hey Jesus.

Man, I can't believe it's taken me so long to get here. Thank you for being so patient and waiting for me.

I know I'm not perfect and have had made enough mistakes to spiritually bankrupt me, but I know that you love me and there's nothing you can't fix.

I'm sorry for everything I've done to hurt you and rebel against you. I'm making a pledge, to commit myself to you and live for you. I know you're the Alpha and Omega - the Lord of all - and I admit that I need you.

I receive the free gift that you are offering me, to live with you forever here on this earth and after. I don't want to be dragged down by the hunters though they will try so hard, I want to live with you and fight on your side.

Please forgive me for everything I have done.

I can't beat porn and lust by myself, I've tried, and I just can't do it. I need you to set me free, because it's only you who can do that. I look to you and to your strength to get out of the hunters' traps and I need you to help me fight for purity.

Please identify and bring healing to the pain in my life, the reason why I've developed these habits in the first place.

I love you. Thank you so much for loving me. Show me your plan and purpose for my life.

Guide me every step of the way and show me how we can take this world back from the hunters and free as many others as possible. Fill me with your spirit and power.

I ask this in the name of Jesus and through the power of the blood that he shed for me on the cross. Amen."

If you made a commitment, then let me be the first to say welcome to the pack!

It's a challenge, but it's the greatest adventure you'll ever embark on.

From here there are a few steps you can take.

1. Start reading the Bible

This is God's word filled with wisdom, truth and stories of men and women from across history who God have done incredible things for God.

It can seem like quite an intimidating text, but I recommend you start with a book in it called John. That way you can read about the life of Jesus for yourself.

Just pick up a free app version or a order physical copy from online.

Personally, I read what's called the NLT version because it's translated into language I find easy to understand and relate to, but any of the most well-known versions will do.

2. Start to pray

People can get all worked up about how to pray.

Honestly, prayer is simply talking to God. You don't need any fancy structure or buzzwords.

Just start talking to God as you would anyone else. Ask him to help you and thank him for your life.

The longer you walk with Him, the more he will be able to speak into your life and guide you.

Start taking the first steps today.

3. Get connected to a local church

Especially one that has a lot of people your age.

That way you can naturally form a Wolfpack and have others to support you along this journey.

I would try Googling 'church near me' then contact them to see if there are many people your age and then go check it out. Ideally, if you know someone who already goes to church, get in touch with them and they will gladly help.

For those of you who didn't make a commitment, thanks so much for bearing with me.

Hopefully the ideas talked about so far have still been of some benefit to you.

But now ladies and gentlemen, it's time for the final section…

VICTORY.

(Why we're doing this in the first place.)

See you there.

STORIES FROM THE WOLFPACK
- Bill Foye: Pastor of Hope Church

Who are you?

I'm Bill Foye, I'm 33 years old and I'm a pastor at Hope Church here in Northern Ireland.

In your opinion what impact do you think porn is having?

I think it's having a massive impact that spills into almost every area of our culture.

For a lot of older people, it's like a dirty secret that no one wants to talk about, yet the stats about how many Christians are consuming it is incredibly high.

So it creates this weird dynamic where we have an issue that is prevalent in our churches that no one wants to talk about.

In terms of the impact, I think the biggest thing is that it distorts our view of reality.

It distorts our relationships with others, but also distorts our relationship with God.

For Christians struggling with an addiction to pornography this distortion can be even more acute... here you have people who are meant to be forgiven, free and liberated from the power of sin yet they can spend years struggling with this stuff.

It's easy to feel like that just doesn't add up.

But the good news is that we are not on our own in feeling like this.

In Romans 7:15, the apostle Paul - one of the most important men in biblical history - confesses this:

"I don't really understand myself, for I want to do what is right, but I don't do it. Instead, I do what I hate."

Christians caught up in a lust addiction can really relate to this summary.

Generally speaking, this isn't just an issue for teenage guys as people have sometimes thought.

It impacts the whole church community; young and old, male and female, people from all sorts of backgrounds and people who are at different stages in life.

Why do you think the church has been silent about this?

The last wave of Christianity, particularly in Northern Ireland, placed a high importance on purity and holiness. It was a major part of their teaching and preaching.

This obviously isn't a bad thing, but a lack of transparency, vulnerability and the harsh judgement of sexual sin led the individuals struggling to cover their issues up and stay silent.

This has led to a 'behind-closed-doors' culture.

So from the outside, it may have looked like all was good and that none of this went on within the church.

Perhaps that suited the church because it allowed them to avoid talking about these issues which are often complex, messy and - for many people - awkward.

But the soil of secrecy, darkness and isolation is a breeding ground for bondage.

Without a doubt, we need to be having conversations around these issues because they are such a big part of our lives and the statistics speak for themselves.

Why do you think so many people are consuming porn?

There are a whole host of reasons why people are consuming this stuff, different people for different reasons, but I have seen these three reasons to be amongst the most common.

1. Easy accessibility
2. Natural drive of human nature (hunger as Matt put it)
3. Dissatisfaction with reality.

I think most people use porn as a way to escape our reality.

There is a real tragedy here, because the more time we spend consuming it, the more it warps our view of reality.

Reality alone is where real beauty, real adventure and real satisfaction can only be found.

Our 21st-century life is very busy, stressful and manic. In a way, porn becomes a drug that we use to 'medicate' ourselves in the midst of our strains, stresses and sores.

Porn can be a quick way to decompress in the short-term, and like most 'drugs' has long-term side effects.

Overdependence + reliance = addiction.

What would you say to someone sitting in your church pews who is a porn addict?

I would say that you are still loved by God.

That the love of God, the forgiveness of God and the smile of God still extends to you.

That this sin that entraps you is no worse than other sins we wrestle with in our lives.

That the heart of God breaks for both the people watching and the people being watched.

That humanity, self-worth and dignity are eroded through porn… for everyone involved.

Both the consumer and the people being consumed are made in the image of God and both are loved.

This absolutely is not God's ideal or desire for anyone.

And I would also want to say that freedom is possible. The gospel of Jesus still works. Salvation is past, present and future.

But also its important to recognise that sexual sin is unique… In 1 Corinthians 6:18 Paul writes *"whoever sins sexually, sins against their own body."* That's something to really think about. It means when we engage in what the Bible calls 'sexual immorality' we are actually pointing the knife inward to ourselves. That's why the fable of the wolf works so well.

That means the longer we engage in it the more damage we are doing to ourselves. God can and does heal wounds and can purify minds and memories but he does not erase reality.

How can Christians experience freedom from this addiction?

Freedom looks different for everyone; some people experience it in a moment, for others it can take a long time. As someone who has walked part of this journey in my own life, I find that turning to the true character of God has been essential.

Reminding myself of who he is by looking at his word, scriptures like Psalm 103, Psalm 51, Psalm 32, Exodus 34 and Micah 7 for example have been real pillars in my own life.

When we're addicted to something like this and we can't break free from it despite praying and crying out to God for freedom, it can actually twist our view of Him.

It can make us feel rejected by God and unloved.

But God's forgiveness is much bigger than our porn problem.

He loves us so deeply, and wants to walk on this journey with us.

Addictions can come and go, but his love and forgiveness is unchanging.

PLUS you are definitely not alone.
There are other people sitting with you in church who are going through the exact same thing.

It's easy to feel like you are the only one, but you certainly aren't.

Discussion questions

1. Have you made a commitment to live life with Jesus? If you have or haven't... why?

2. Do you feel guilt or shame surrounding the issue of porn? Where do you think that comes from?

3. Why do we hide away from God when we sin? What can we do to flip that on it's head and learn to run towards him instead?

4. What's your biggest takeaway from Bill's story?

VICTORY

Chapter 13 - Why fight?

Here we are guys, the final stretch is in sight.

Hopefully what we have covered so far has given you a lot to think about.

We're almost done, and I just have a few more key points to share.

This one is important because it deals with why we fight.

Without solid reasons to embark on this journey, you will lose motivation quickly in the battle.

Knowing your *why* helps you push on and keep going, even when it seems like you aren't getting anywhere.

You will have your own list of *why's*. Here are a few of mine.

These are the reasons I fought through my teens and continue to fight today.

1. Self-control

Frankly, I don't want to go through life living with a habit or personality trait that I have no control over.

I think we are all responsible for our own actions and if I don't have strong self-control over my body then I see myself as a liability for the people I come in contact with and an easy target for the hunters.

How many cases of sexual abuse could be avoided if the perpetrator involved had control over themselves?

How many of these situations are rooted in a history of pornography and self-gratification?

I ask these questions sensitively and genuinely.

2. Sex-life

Let's keep it real. I wanted to have a great sex life. Few things hurt that more than an addiction to pornography and/or masturbation.

3. For my wife

(Disclaimer: I am pro-marriage but also believe singleness is equally as incredible. If marriage isn't for you, don't exclude yourself from this. Family comes in many shapes and forms.)

One of the things that really motivated me as a 16-year-old to beat my addiction was to it do for my future family.

What's cool is that many young fighters I meet today also have this as a key motivating reason for why they fight.

I wanted my wife to be able to trust me, I wanted her to know that she is the only woman I would have eyes for and open myself up to intimately.

Those are impossible commitments to make if I'm engaging with other women from all over the world through pornography.

I knew I was only going to have the ability to make those promises to her when I was free.

Now I am married I am so beyond thankful to be free. Jaci continually expresses how difficult it would have been for her if I wasn't.

We know several couples who are going through really tough times in their marriage due to a partner having an unhealthy relationship with porn.

The hurt and distrust it can cause in a marriage is staggering, and while we believe 100% that couples in this situation can get through it, we want to help prevent people from ever making it that far (hence the book.)

4. For my sons and daughters

I didn't have any kids when I was 16 (and I still don't,) but I keep them in mind and use them as a motivation to fight for purity.

Here's why:

- Porn objectifies women: There's just no way around that. I for one don't want my daughters to be objectified nor do I want my sons to be the ones doing the objectifying. (**Note:** I know it works the other way round too, don't worry.)

- I don't want my kids to be trapped like I was.

- I want to be part of the change so that they live in a better world. Human trafficking, prostitution, rape, teen pregnancies, low self-worth, isolation, depression and even paedophilia I firmly believe are connected to the porn industry and lust related issues. I don't want any of my kids to be caught up in any of this.

5. To fight against human trafficking

Over the years I have been involved in a variety of anti-human trafficking efforts.

Human trafficking is basically modern day slavery, it's a blanket statement to describe forced labour, child labour, underpaid work, organ harvesting and sex slavery (being forced to have sex with someone for money.)

You'll often hear that human trafficking is made up of a triangle because it requires 3 parts to exist.

Let's take the sex industry as an example.

- **The pimp:** the man/woman/group that runs the brothel and enslaves the product.

- **The product:** the man/woman/child who is lured, abducted or groomed into the sex industry.

- **The customer:** the man/woman who gives money to the pimp to use (abuse) the product.

All it takes to end human trafficking is to remove one part of the triangle, and the whole industry will fall apart.

E.g. If there are no pimps then there are no brothels. If are no people enslaved then there is nothing to sell but most importantly: If there are no customers, there will be no business.

Pimps are hard to reach. They are underground and/or are untouchable by the law. Whether they are walking the streets or sitting in a corporate office.

The product is also hard to reach because these people are either hidden under lock and key or are often ensnared by drugs or psychological abuse.

The customers however are easy to reach. They are the people we see in the street, the people we work with and the people we go to school with.

But most of all, they are the people we see in the mirror.
If we can take the customer out of the equation, the whole industry collapses.

Human trafficking and the porn industry is a business just like any other, it's built on the principle of supply and demand.

If we cut the demand, then the industry implodes.

That's why this matters. It is only through a cultural revolution that we can defeat these industries, and it starts with us.

It starts with our friendship groups, our neighbourhood, our city, town or village. We have the opportunity to raise kids and raise up a generation that will say this is wrong, that enough is enough.

But first, it starts with us. It starts with me, and it starts with you.

When I first heard about human trafficking, it broke my heart. My blood boiled against those who would abuse other humans in such a grotesque way.

Imagine the shock I felt when God tapped me on the shoulder and showed me how my hands were far from clean. How by consuming pornography I was feeding into this triangle.

I realised that before going off and railing against the people behind these industries, I had to first remove the plank in my own eye.

Change must start internally. We must cut off the demand.

This is why we fight. There's too much on the line for us not to.

6. To run towards my purpose

It's clear by now that I believe in God and I believe that he has a purpose for every single one of us.

I believe these purposes bring 'the kingdom of heaven here on earth.'

That just means to make our world, neighbourhoods and cities more like heaven.

For me in this season that means encouraging people to overcome their addictions to porn.

For Scott Harrison and the team at Charity Water, that means creating access to clean water for people in parts of the world who don't.

For Petey K and the team at No More Traffik it is to end Human Trafficking.

For David Johnston and the team at OutsideIn it's to rewrite the story of homelessness.

Many of you will choose to become a school teacher to raise up a generation.

Others interpret that as going into medicine to find a cure for diseases that will save thousands of lives.

Heck, a few of you reading could see this as releasing the greatest rock album of all time.

We all have something - 'our thing' - a purpose.

Being free helps us take our place and do our bit to change the world. The hunters love to burden us down and take our eyes off the prize and lust is an easy way for them to do that.

We all have a part to play in the Alpha's plan, and the good news is that we aren't alone. I believe we are being watched and cheered on by those who have gone before.

"Therefore, since we are surrounded by such a huge crowd of witnesses to the life of faith, let us strip off every weight that slows us down, especially the sin that so easily trips us up. And let us run with endurance the race God has set before us." - Hebrews 12:1

I know that we can do amazing things with the short life we are given, and my hope is that our generation will put down our distractions and apathy to run after a full, purpose-driven life.

7. Because freed people free people

Freedom is infectious. Once you experience it, you won't be content to keep it to yourself.

Not only will you become a *"yeah me too"* voice in someone's life but you can offer hope by saying *"but not anymore, I've been there yeah, but I can tell you that there is a way out of this and freedom is possible."*

This sounds very idyllic, but it's no fairy tale.

If this book has done anything, I pray that it has filled you with hope but also grounded you in the reality that while this is not easy and takes a lot of guts, it is absolutely worth it.

This is why we fight. Every single day.

Sometimes we win, sometimes we lose, but that doesn't matter. What matters is that we show up.

What matters is that you start this journey if you never have.

What matters is that you pick yourself up again even if it's the 150th time you've tried.

What matters is that I finish typing out this page.

What matters is that we step up and run fiercely towards the purposes God has put us here to do.

True victory belongs to the one who fights.

To the man or woman in the arena.

It doesn't matter how many times you fail.

What matters is that you fight.

Spoiler alert: you can do it.

STORIES FROM THE WOLFPACK
- Peter Kernoghan: No More Traffik

Who are you?

My name is Peter Kernoghan; an activist, passionate about social change specifically when it comes to fairness.

I'm the Development Director and Founder of a charity called No More Traffik.

Put simply; we are a movement of people and communities committed to stopping human trafficking both locally in Northern Ireland and globally.

What's the link between porn and human trafficking?

It's important to make this clear: there's no data that concretely links porn and human trafficking together.

They are, however, pieces of the puzzle that when you connect together reveal the full picture of how we as a society devalue ourselves and each other.

What impact do you think porn is having on our society?

I think it strips the value out of people.

Every individual has value and anything that strips away human value is something that we as a culture should push back on.

Porn is ultimately about self-gratification. It turns the people on the screen into a commodity and something to be consumed therefore devaluing them...

But it also devalues us when we watch.

You see healthy relationships are all about adding value to others... Porn flips that on its head. It's a one-way transaction.

The fact that it is so mass-market, so accessible and so widely accepted tells a story about where we truly are as a culture.

I think this is interesting considering how we pride ourselves on being so progressive and boasting that we have come so far, often turning our noses up at the slavery of the past only to engage in the slavery of the present.

How does porn impact sex?

Porn is an unrealistic depiction of sex because it is usually driven through the lens of male-gratification.

Real-life, healthy sexual relationships don't work that way. The purpose of sex is putting your spouse's needs above your own, not just seeking your own pleasure.

Knowing what you know, how does it change the way you raise your kids?

For me, it's all about establishing a healthy relationship with technology and devices.

We teach our kids that phones, tablets and computers are tools designed to help us carry out a specific purpose. We don't get devices because we NEED them. We use them because they can help us.

If the purpose doesn't exist, then we shouldn't use the device. If they hurt us more than they help us, then we simply shouldn't use them.

For example, my 8-year-old really wants a phone so she can message with her friends... but the reality is, there's no real purpose for that at this stage of her life.

That'll change of course when she starts to go out by herself and needs a way to communicate with us, but too often (adults included) we mindlessly add tech to our lives.

The reality is, like most tools, they have great potential for good, but if used incorrectly they can bring a lot of harm.

The internet and social media and devices aren't evil, but they can be used for evil and it's important we protect our kids (and ourselves) from those evils.

What do you think the next step for porn is?

I think the next step will be user-generated content.

I was speaking to someone the other day and they were saying that young people no longer need to access porn because they generate their own.

In the age of YouTube and SnapChat and Instagram we have all become content creators, when you add this to a high-school environment highly fueled by porn then of course that's what's going to happen.

That and virtual reality.

Discussion questions

1. Why do/will you fight?

2. What can you look forward to in the future when you overcome your current habits?

3. How can you support other people along in this journey?

4. What's your biggest takeaway from Peter's story?

Chapter 14 - Dealing With Discouragement

"Wow really dude... You're going to talk about failure in the victory section? That's whack."

Yeah 'dude.' You know what else is whack?

Being sold a lie.

The journey to freedom is not as simple as a '7 step program' or a '30 day routine - it's a lifelong commitment.

By committing to beat this thing you are committing to getting back up again and again and again and again.

That's what a true fighter is.

If a UFC fighter gave up their career every time they got knocked down, they wouldn't even make it through their first training session.

As the old saying goes: *"It's not the size of the dog in the fight, but it's the size of the fight in the dog."*

You will make mistakes, you will face discouragement. But you will get there.

Spirals

It's easy to feel like you are stuck in a cycle…

- you make a commitment - have a good streak - relapse - binge - feel guilty - recommit - start again -

It can feel like you are destined to run in circles forever.

A friend once told me to think of this cycle not as a flat 2D circle but rather a 3D spring or spiral.

Like walking up a spiral staircase.

While you may be walking round and round in circles, progress is actually being made with each step, moving you up, eventually bringing you to the top and out of the cycle.

Each time you commit to getting on that staircase you refuse to stay where you are, you choose to move forward and someday you will make it to the top.

The hunters love to try and convince us that once we relapse all of our progress is wasted and we're back to square one.

Don't fall for it.

They do this to try and stop us from getting back on the staircase.

To make us binge and discredit how far we've come. Whether it's one day, one month, one week or one year, GET UP, dust yourself off and keep fighting.

That's the last thing you'll want to do, but it's the only way you'll make it.

Dealing with discouragement from other people

Discouragement comes in all shapes and forms.
In the process of overcoming my addiction and writing this book, I've had backlashes from strangers, friends and even family members.

The first time I publicly spoke out against pornography it was met with: *"this isn't appropriate, remove this right now, think of the shame it will bring."*

The first time I shared the message of *The Blood Tipped Blade* I had close friends criticising me over text while I was speaking onstage.

I've had people tell me I'm bigoted, stiff, anti-sex, no fun and labelled as just another crazy Christian.

I've had people tell me when I was trying to overcome my addiction that I would never be able to beat it because 'that's just the way guys are' and that it's perfectly natural and healthy.

Don't expect people to rally around you and cheer you on - but don't hate them when they don't.

Understand that it can be hard for people, especially older generations to understand if it was something they themselves didn't experience.

Understand that there is still a massive taboo surrounding issues like this in a lot of parts of the world.

Give grace for the confusion that some people will have and recognise the hunters will try to do anything to discourage you.

You have to know why you are doing this and you have to hold onto that.

Block out the haters, stick to your Wolfpack.
Block out the hunters, listen to the Alpha.

All of us are on a journey in life. Don't let the words or attitudes of others derail you from yours.

Learn the meaning of grace

Nothing will show you how much you need grace more than this journey.

It'll show you that you can't do it on your own.

It'll show you that you are not and never will be perfect.

It'll show you that you have no right to judge anyone.

But it will show you that God loves you anyway.

Once you grasp that it will change your faith.

You will learn to show more grace to the people around you and most difficult of all, you will learn how to show grace to yourself.

STORIES FROM THE WOLFPACK
- Becky Kaskel: Full-time ministry worker

Who are you?

My name is Becky Kaskel and I'm a 25-year-old living in New York City!

I'm a daughter to great loving parents, a sister to the 2 best brothers and a friend to some pretty incredible people from all over the world.

My interests include long walks on the beach, reading a good book by the fire and pepperoni pizza.

Haha ok, maybe sometimes it's just the pizza.

When did your journey with lust begin?

I first found myself in the grips of addiction when I was young - too young to remember how it even started.

For 15 years I sat on the edge of my seat waiting for someone to bring it up, hoping that they would meet me in the middle.

Lust is tough because it hides so well.

For my whole life, I've been involved in worship, drama, youth groups, missions trips, preaching, writing and leading all while keeping a secret I so desperately wanted to escape from.

Though I've been in ministry for over 10 years, I only recently began to find freedom.

If you've been struggling and hiding and hoping and waiting, you're not alone.

Is lust just a guys issue?

When I was 19, I went on a retreat weekend that my sister-in-law had asked me to attend.

My friend, Mercedes sponsored the cost for me to go, and she even picked me up and took me to dinner before the first session began.

God was going to do something in my life that weekend, and she knew it.

One of the evening sessions was a sort-of representation of dying to sin.

I walked with 20 women I didn't know into a big room where there was a wooden cross.

They asked us to write down our shortcomings, struggles, and fears. Anything that we needed to let go of, we were to nail to the cross.

One by one, we would go up, read our paper, and then nail it onto the wood. I was a little squinty-eyed, wondering what this was going to change, but I gave in.

I wrote some words down that I had never even said aloud before.

When it came time to start sharing, I got up first, sat in front of the cross, and began to read. I stared at my sheet the entire time, hoping that I wouldn't implode under the weight of my embarrassment.

I finished reading, nailed my paper to the cross, stood up, and looked around the room. Everyone was crying. I mean, everyone.

One by one, other women walked to the cross and shared about their own battles with lust.

I was amazed.

Girls, please, if nothing else, hear me when I say, you're not the only one.

Some girls think about sex a lot. Other girls battle porn. Many girls are bound by lust.

And you know what, that's just as 'normal' as any boy struggling with the same. It's not somehow different or worse because simply because you're female.

Sin is sin, and the enemy is after us all.

Don't let the lie of thinking that 'lust is just a guy's issue' further bind you in your battle.

How important is it to speak out?

I remember the first time I heard another girl speak up about her battle with lust.

I was in my first year of college at a Christian gathering called Cru.

This particular night, the leaders had set up a microphone in the front of the room, encouraging an open mic night of sorts. They called it Testimony Night.

A few people shared their stories before she got up to speak. In all honesty, I don't remember her story.

What I do remember though is that once she finished, she spoke to the room and asked everyone who struggled with lust to stand up.

Fear. That's all I felt.

It had been 15 years of hiding and waiting and hurting, and when the moment finally came, I was terrified.

One by one, I watched other people stand up. In that moment, I fought 15 years of thoughts and fears to get out of my seat. Everyone clapped for us.

I didn't realise it then, but that's where my path to freedom really started.

So, why should you speak out? In James, scripture tells us that confessing our sins one to another leads to healing, and I don't think that verse was written by accident.

I believe that God forgives us of our sins and that there is grace upon grace for each and every one of us.

But there is a very real shift that takes place when you speak up to someone.

If you've prayed the same prayer a million times and still feel like your sin is a scar to hide behind, speak up. I promise, there is healing waiting for you.

The best part? You never know who's listening.

I waited 15 years to get out of my seat and maybe one day you'll be the voice that helps someone to get out of theirs.

What would you say to encourage the 16-year-old version of yourself?

1. Speak up.

No one else is talking about it? Maybe they're waiting for you to.

All it takes is one word to start to start a conversation.

Ask questions. Read. Journal. Get your thoughts out of your head. Fighting the secret is half of your battle. It's amazing how much easier it is to fight when there are other people taking up the sword with you.

2. Don't kiss him.

It might seem like it's no big deal right now, but all of those "one thing led to another" moments will leave you broken.

Love is not merely physical.

Put safeguards up around your heart, listen to your parents' guidance, and stop letting boys have so much of you. Learn about you, what you desire, and what you deserve, and don't stop for anyone on the way.

It really is possible for God to be enough.

3. Take a deep breath.

The only thing that is forever is Jesus.

It may feel like you're going to crumble but remember...

You are not alone.

Discussion questions

1. How can you prepare yourself for discouraging times?

2. How can you show grace to people struggling and why should you?

3. What will you do after messing up after a good win streak? Write down things you will do, people you will call etc...

4. What's your biggest takeaway from Becky's story?

Chapter 15 - Keep on fighting

"Be who you needed when you were younger." - Ayesha Siddiqi

That's it guys. 15 chapters later and we've made it. Matthew has officially run out of things to say.

Thanks for coming on this journey with me.

I'm a big fan of the quote *"be who you needed when you were younger."* (If you're stuck on your purpose that's a good place to start.)

For me that spun into *'write the book you needed to read when you were younger'* and that's exactly what The Blood Tipped Blade has become.

I wrote this book for 16-year-old Matthew in the best way I knew how.

It's far from perfect, but that's what future editions are for, right?

At points it rambles, the gramamr isn't perfect and all the commas aren't in the right place. But it's a start and I know that my

Wolfpack and I would have appreciated this book 7 years ago...

Even if it was just to hear a "me too," see that freedom is possible and have loads of things to discuss/debate about.
You see, I believe with all my heart that God is raising up a generation of fighters who won't be afraid to stand up and take their place.

Young men and women who won't run away from the purposes and plans he has placed inside of them that will ultimately lead to changing the world.

The Blood Tipped Blade can represent a lot of things in our lives that hold us back from reaching our true potential.

Hopefully, this book has given you a few ideas of how to tackle them.

It's my prayer that you're brave enough to run after and fight for the purposes God put you on this world for.

But always remember: *the choice is yours.*

- Matthew

Action steps

What's next for you? What steps do you need to take after reading this book? A change to your home? Friendship groups? Daily routines? Conversations you need to have? People you want to send this book to? Write them here, then tick them off as you complete them.

A Round Of Applause For...

My wonderful wife Jaci. Thank you for loving me so well and being my #1 supporter. Marrying you has made all of THE FIGHT worth it and I'm so greatful I get to live out this adventure with you.

To the Wolfpack of my teens and beyond, specifically Steve, Nathan, Robin and Pete. You guys have been there for me when I needed you most and love you all like the brothers I never had.

Bill, Dave, Andrew and Jamie. You guys stepped in as older role models at such a critical stage of my life. I am forever grateful.

All of the amazing contributors who shared their stories with us. Anghell, Ross, Nils, Jeff, Jaci, Rebecca, Mum, Steve, Bill, Brad, Rob, Petey K and of course Becky! You have breathed life into this project and injected it with such courage and diversity that I could never have achieved on my own.

Jeff, you have been a backbone for this book that I have leaned on so many times in many different ways. I only hope that I can be as helpful when you come to publishing your first book (you have to do it now!)

Nils, you get a special mention because you were the first person I told about this project and bounced the early concept and outline off! Thanks for all you have done for me personally and for this book, especially your story and epic illustration. I love you like a brother.

Mum + Merdy. Thanks so much for all your support and chats around the dinner table. So excited to see where God takes you in this next season of your life.

To all of our incredible Kickstarter backers, with special thanks to Jonny Murray! You guys made this happen! Thanks for taking a risk and backing this project, your support has been essential both financially and emotionally.

It may be a cliche, but Jesus, without you I wouldn't even be here. Every dark valley and every sunny mountaintop you've been there. I can't believe that we finally got this book out there, thanks for sticking with me and for guiding me the way you did. Sorry for freaking out so many times.

Last but certainly not least, thank you for reading. I pray that any good from this book sticks with you and that the rest falls away.

About The Author

I've shared enough about me in this book already, don't you think?

All money generated by this project is pumped straight back into getting as many people to read it as possible *(except 10% which is donated to No More Traffik to support the incredible work they do.)*

To enquire about bulk buying copies of this book, stocking it in your shop, booking speaking gigs, donating to the cause or any other 'businessy' stuff please email matthewtbelfast@gmail.com

The goal is to get this message out there to the people who need it most and I really appreciate any way you can help make this happen.

For now, this is my first and only book, but I'm hard at work trying to change that.

(Don't worry, it's not about porn.)

The Next Step Of The Journey

I'm always up to something, and the best place to find out what's happening is via my website.

From there you can check out my other projects, tune into one of my podcasts and sign-up to a free email newsletter.

I spend a lot of time working on devotionals, essays and podcasts to help people live simple lives full of freedom and purpose.

Would really love for you to be a part of the next chapter.

Check out: https://matthewthompson.org

Spread The Word

If you've enjoyed this book, I'd really appreciate it if you could give it a review on Amazon.

It's dead easy and only takes 2 minutes.

(Just search 'The Blood Tipped Blade' on Amazon).

I know you probably hear authors say this a lot, but it helps the book reach more new people than you'd think.

Lastly, if you share the book on your social media page, blog, website, group, forum, etc - I would appreciate it so much.

Thanks again.

- Matthew

P.S. Shoot an email to matthewtbelfast@gmail.com if you wanna say hi (I just deleted all my social media).

38281262R00157

Printed in Poland
by Amazon Fulfillment
Poland Sp. z o.o., Wrocław